Broken Roads, Strong Hearts

Broken Roads, Strong Hearts

LIFE LESSONS ON LOVE, RESILIENCE, AND RENEWAL

GEORGE HATCHER

CasaHatcherPress

For Molly — the heart behind every word, and the proof that real love endures.

"Real love is not the firework that dazzles, but the pilot light that endures." — George Hatcher

Broken Roads, Strong Hearts: Life Lessons on Love, Resilience, and Renewal

This volume contains the following previously published works by George Hatcher:

Fake Love (First edition August 2025)

Love Is What It Is: Lessons From Everyday Life (First edition September 2025)

Ignite Your Potential: Break Free From the Ordinary (First edition July 2025)

All three works appear here in their entirety as part of this collected edition.

Published by Casa Hatcher Press, a subsidiary of Pretty Face, Inc.

Rancho Mirage, California 92270

http://casahatcherpress.com

(800) 416-6189

First collected edition, September 2025

ISBN: 979-8-9996764-1-2 (Paperback)

ISBN: 979-8-9996764-2-9 (eBook)

Library of Congress Control Number: Pending

Book and cover design by Casa Hatcher Press

Printed in the United States of America and abroad

Contents

Preface   xi

FAKE LOVE
GEORGE HATCHER

Introduction: A Note from an Imperfect Man   3
1. Chapter 1: The Great Love Hoax   9
2. Chapter 2: Lust at First Sight   13
3. Chapter 3: Surface Tension   17
4. Chapter 4: The Showdown: Learning the
   Difference   21
5. Chapter 5: Fairy Tales and Follies   25
6. Chapter 6: Authenticity in the Age of Filters   29
7. Chapter 7: The Road to Real   33
8. Chapter 8: Embracing Imperfection   37
9. Chapter 9: Conclusion: The only Takeaway That
   Matters   40

LOVE IS WHAT IT IS
GEORGE J HATCHER

1. The Awkward First Date   47
2. The Rollercoaster of Relationships   49
3. Love Languages: The Dialects of Affection   54
4. Communication: The Love Signal   59
5. The Family Factor   64
6. The Friends' Influence   69
7. The Mundane Moments   74
8. Love in the Digital Age   79
9. Lessons Learned the Hard Way   84
10. The Joy of Lasting Love   89

IGNITE YOUR POTENTIAL
GEORGE HATCHER

Introduction   97

1. Chapter 1: Awakening the Fire Within   103
2. Chapter 2: Shifting Your Mindset   106
3. Chapter 3: Setting Meaningful Goals   109
4. Chapter 4: Building Resilience   112
5. Chapter 5: Breaking Free From Routine   115
6. Chapter 6: Harnessing Your Passion   118
7. Chapter 7: Surrounding Yourself with Positivity   121
8. Chapter 8: Taking Action   124
9. Chapter 9: Embracing Lifelong Learning   127
10. Chapter 10: Living a Meaningful Life   130
11. Chapter 11: Reflecting and Reassessing   133
12. Chapter 12: Sustaining Your Momentum   136

Afterword   139
About the Author   141
Also by George Hatcher   143

Preface

When I look back at my life, it doesn't read like one smooth story — it reads like several books bound together. There were the early chapters, filled with ambition, mistakes, and hard lessons learned the long way. There were chapters about love — both the kind that breaks apart quickly and the kind that holds you steady for sixty years. And there were chapters about finding purpose, reinventing myself, and learning how to build a life that is real and meaningful, even after the storms.

This bundle of three books is my attempt to bring those threads together.

The first book, *Fake Love,* is about the difference between what falls apart and what holds fast. It is the most personal of the three, drawn directly from my marriage to Molly, the woman who stood by me when the fire of my mistakes nearly burned our lives to the ground. That book explores not only the illusions of "fake" love but the miracle of a love that endures.

The second book, *Love Is What It Is,* shifts the lens. It takes us out of the extraordinary crises and into the everyday. Because love is not just in the dramatic gestures — it's in the small, daily acts, the lessons we can notice if we are willing to pay attention. I wanted to capture the wisdom of those ordinary moments, because they are often the most extraordinary of all.

The third book, *Ignite Your Potential*, is about what happens after you've learned those lessons. Once you know what real love feels like, once you've seen how it can reshape your life, the question becomes: how do you carry that forward into everything you do? This book is about motivation, resilience, and the power to live fully and authentically.

Together, these three works form one continuous journey — from love, to lessons, to life. My hope is that by reading them in this order, you will see the connections as I see them: that love is the root, wisdom is the trunk, and a meaningful life is the branches that grow outward.

I don't pretend to be an expert or a guru. I am, as I've often said, an imperfect man. But I've lived through enough brokenness and enough repair to know this much: there is beauty in the cracks, strength in the second chance, and hope in the ordinary.

If you find yourself in these pages, know this — you are not alone in your struggles, and you are never too far gone to begin again.

With gratitude,
George Hatcher

FAKE LOVE

GEORGE HATCHER

Introduction: A Note from an Imperfect Man

Let me be clear right from the start: I am not an expert on love. I'm not a therapist or a guru, and I have no interest in pointing fingers or telling anyone how to live their life. I can only speak from my own experience, and what a wild experience it's been.

The fact that my wife, Molly, and I have been married since 1965 is nothing short of a miracle. I say that because for the first half of our life together, I was a mess. I made mistakes—big ones. My ambition often outpaced my resources, leading to a series of business failures and white-collar crimes that landed me in jail not once, but several times. I was a wild person, and through it all—the bad checks, the court dates, the 42 months I eventually served for false bank entries—Molly waited for me. She was there. Always.

This book is about the difference between a love that endures and one that shatters at the first sign of trouble. I know that difference intimately. Before Molly, I was married three times; one of those marriages lasted just 24 days. I know what it's like when things fall apart. But my life with Molly has taught me what it means to hold things together. The love I have for her, and she for me, is the reason we survived the storms that would have, and should have, wrecked us. It's the anchor that allowed for the "miracle turn-around" in the second, much cleaner and happier, half of our life.

So when I talk about "fake love" in these pages, I'm not judging anyone. Many people in such relationships might already know it. I'm simply exploring the contrast. What I call "fake love" is fragile. It's the relationship that ends at the first argument, the first financial struggle, the first real test. Real love, as I've been blessed to experience it, is something else entirely. It's the force that withstands failure, humiliation, and even prison bars. It's the bedrock that remains when everything else has been washed away.

This book is my attempt to explore that difference. It's a collection of observations from an imperfect man who, by some grace, found a love so real it saw him through the worst of himself and into the best of his life.

To Molly, who showed me the difference between what fades and what endures.

Chapter 1: The Great Love Hoax

With the story you've just read in the introduction, you can understand why my 60-year partnership with Molly feels like it was forged in fire. The love we share isn't a fairy tale; it's the sturdy, time-tested reality that serves as my anchor.

That's why, when I look at the landscape of modern dating, I feel like I'm looking at a different planet. It seems to be a world of what I can only call 'fake love'—a grand and glittering hoax. It's a fast-paced game of fleeting distractions and superficial connections, and frankly, it looks exhausting. From the vantage point of a love that has survived everything, the whole endeavor seems designed to leave people feeling more alone than ever.

The Heart's Deceptions in a World of Swipes

· · ·

The game often starts with what I'm told is the "Tinder trap." It promises endless potential connections right at your fingertips, but what it often delivers is a series of interactions that lack any real depth. It's the illusion that the next best thing is just a swipe away, so why invest in the person right in front of you? People find themselves on a carousel of awkward dates and mismatched expectations, all while chasing the high of a new match.

The problem is, this system encourages us to confuse a biological spark with a genuine connection. It's easy to mistake lust for love when you're judging a person based on a handful of perfectly curated photos and a clever one-liner. Lust is the flash of lightning; it's exciting and immediate. Love is the slow, steady rain that follows, the kind that actually nourishes the ground so something real can grow. In this modern game, it seems many are so busy chasing the lightning that they never stick around long enough for the rain.

Love in the Age of Disappearing Acts

This brings me to another phenomenon that baffles me: ghosting. In my day, if you weren't interested, you had the decency (or at least the courage) to say so. Now, people simply vanish without a trace, like a magician's disappearing act. One minute you're sharing memes and flirty texts, and the next you're left wondering if the whole thing was a figment of your imagination.

This isn't just about bad manners; it's a symptom of a culture that treats people as disposable. These disappearing acts are the natural consequence of surface-level relationships. When a connection has no roots, there's nothing to hold it in place. It fosters an environment of fake affection where authenticity is the first casualty. How can you build trust with someone if you're half-expecting them to become a ghost? Real love is about showing up, staying present, and choosing to work through things—not just vanishing when it gets inconvenient.

A Chapter 1 Reflection: Unmasking Your Own Search

Before we go further, it's worth taking a moment to think about this. The first step in avoiding a trap is knowing you're in one. Ask yourself:

1 What am I *really* looking for? Is it a temporary distraction and a bit of fun, or am I genuinely seeking a deep and meaningful connection? There is no wrong answer, but being honest with yourself is the most important first step.

2 When have I felt most authentic in a relationship (of any kind)? What were the circumstances? What did it feel like to show your true self, imperfections and all?

3 In my own actions, how do I distinguish between love and lust? How do I treat people when I'm simply infatuated versus when I truly care for their well-being?

. . .

Thinking about these questions won't magically solve the problem, but it will give you a compass. In a world selling a fantasy, the most powerful thing you can do is get clear on your own reality. In the next chapter, we'll look closer at the "hotness factor" and how prioritizing looks can be the first, and most deceptive, step in this great love hoax.

Chapter 2: Lust at First Sight

Believe me, I understand lust. In my younger days, before I learned the difference between a thrill and a foundation, I chased my share of shiny objects. I know firsthand how a pretty face or a spark of chemistry can feel like the most important thing in the world. It's a powerful, intoxicating force. But I also know, from the wreckage of three failed marriages, that it's a terrible architect. You can't build a life on a flash of lightning; you need something that will stand up to the storm.

Lust at first sight is where the great love hoax often begins. It's the easiest trap to fall into because it's biological. It's exciting. It's a roller coaster that's all thrilling drops and no slow, steady climb. But the ride always ends, and if that's all there is to the connection, you're left standing on the platform, a little dizzy and alone.

The Hotness Factor and the Chemistry Conundrum

. . .

In today's world, it seems this initial spark is everything. The "hotness factor" reigns supreme. People meticulously curate their appearances online, and we're conditioned to swipe right on the most polished profiles. It's the allure of being seen with someone deemed 'hot'. But what does that really get you? In my experience, a relationship built only on looks is like ordering a beautifully plated dish at a fancy restaurant only to discover that it tastes like cardboard. The excitement fades, and you're left craving something with actual substance.

What I find beautiful in Molly after 60 years has very little to do with the snapshot of the woman I married in 1965. The beauty I see now is in the lines around her eyes that map our shared laughter and tears. It's in the comfort of her presence that got me through my darkest days. That kind of beauty doesn't fade; it deepens. It's a beauty you'll never find if you're only chasing the "hotness factor."

The same goes for that elusive thing people call "chemistry." It can feel like a magical, sugary rush that sweeps you off your feet. But a sugar rush inevitably leads to a crash. Many of my early mistakes in relationships were built on that rush—confusing a fleeting, biological reaction with a true emotional bond. When the passion is all-consuming, it can blind you to the fact that you have nothing in common, no shared values, and no ability to communicate when things get tough. A real, lasting connection isn't a sugar rush; it's a slow-cooked meal. It takes time, patience, and the right ingredients to develop a rich and satisfying flavor.

Love's Awkward Little Brother: "Friends with Benefits"

. . .

This modern idea of "friends with benefits" strikes me as another offshoot of this confusion—a fiasco born from prioritizing lust while pretending it's something more convenient. It's an attempt to get the physical intimacy of a relationship without any of the vulnerability, commitment, or emotional heavy lifting.

But intimacy is more than an act; it's a state of being. It's about knowing and being known. When you try to isolate the physical part, you often end up with a connection that leaves you feeling more empty than satisfied. It's like trying to have a fireplace that gives off heat with no fire. It misses the entire point. In a true partnership, physical affection is an expression of a much deeper bond —a bond of trust, respect, and shared history. It's not the foundation; it's one of the beautiful rooms in a house that you've built together.

A Chapter 2 Reflection: Looking Beyond the Spark

If you want to build something that lasts, you have to be able to see beyond that initial, blinding spark of lust. Take a moment to ask yourself:

1 What qualities, beyond physical appearance, do I find genuinely and lastingly attractive in a person? Think about character, humor, kindness, or intelligence.

2 Think of a time you felt strong "chemistry" with someone. What was it really made of? Was it just physical attraction, or was it a shared sense of humor, intellectual excitement, or emotional understanding?

3 What does emotional intimacy mean to you? How does it differ from physical intimacy, and what role do you want both to play in your life?

Learning to distinguish the flash of lust from the steady glow of love is a crucial skill. It's the difference between chasing a firefly and navigating by the North Star. One is a fleeting distraction; the other can guide you home.

Chapter 3: Surface Tension

～

In my day, you got to know a person face-to-face. You learned about them through their stories, their handshake, the way their eyes lit up when they talked about something they loved. There were no online profiles to manage, no photo filters to apply. The only "highlight reel" was the memories you built together, good and bad.

Today, it seems we live in an age of immense surface tension. Everyone is curating a perfect public image, especially when it comes to relationships. This creates a pressure to live up to an impossible ideal, a myth of perfection that can make real, messy, beautiful love feel inadequate. It's a world built on glittering surfaces, and the tension comes from the fear that one wrong move, one crack in the facade, will cause the whole thing to shatter.

Instagram vs. Reality: The Perfect Relationship Myth

. . .

If Molly and I had social media in the early years of our marriage, our life wouldn't have looked like the perfect couples you see on Instagram. You wouldn't have seen pictures of us on exotic vacations with flawless tans and witty captions. You would have seen the harsh reality of struggle: Molly waiting for me outside a county jail, us trying to rebuild after one of my business ventures imploded. That was our reality. It wasn't pretty, and it certainly wasn't perfect.

This is the danger of the "perfect relationship myth." We scroll through feeds filled with curated moments—the sunset kiss, the anniversary dinner, the laughing selfie—and we mistake that for the whole story. It's a facade. Real life happens between those snapshots. It's in the arguments and the compromises. It's in the quiet, un-photogenic moments of support when one person is falling apart and the other is there to hold them up. Love isn't a highlight reel. It's the raw, unedited footage of a life shared, and chasing an illusion will only leave you feeling hollow when the cameras are off.

The Shiny Object Syndrome

I know a thing or two about chasing the "next big thing." In my business life, it nearly destroyed me. I was always pursuing the next shiny object, the can't-miss deal that I was sure would be the one, and that chase led me down a road of bad decisions and, eventually, to a prison cell. I learned the hard way that the things that glitter the most are rarely gold.

I see the same destructive impulse in modern dating. People are constantly looking over their partner's shoulder for someone newer, more exciting, or "better." It's the "shiny object syndrome" applied to human hearts. But a relationship isn't a trend you can trade in for a new model. A real partnership is something you build, brick by painful, loving brick, over time. It's an investment. By constantly chasing the next thrill, you never give anything real a chance to grow. The greatest treasure of my life wasn't a business deal; it was the woman who stayed, the one who proved that her value was in her steadfastness, not her novelty.

A Chapter 3 Reflection: Breaking the Surface

Escaping the pull of the superficial requires an honest look at what you're chasing and what you're afraid of. Ask yourself:

1 How does the life I present online compare to the one I actually live? In what ways am I curating an image for others?

2 What "shiny objects" (people, lifestyles, possessions) tend to distract me? What am I hoping to find in them that might be missing in my life right now?

3 What am I most afraid of showing to a potential partner? What are the "imperfect" parts of my story that I try to hide? Could those be the very things that allow a real connection to form?

True connection doesn't happen on the surface. It happens when we have the courage to break that tension, to let people see the messy, complicated, and authentic reality underneath. It's a risk, but it's the only way to find a love that's real enough to last.

Chapter 4: The Showdown: Learning the Difference

⌐∾∾⌐

If there is one lesson that has taken me a lifetime to learn, it's this: you must understand the difference between love and lust. Confusing the two is like mistaking a firework for a star. One is a spectacular, noisy explosion that lights up the night for a brilliant moment and then vanishes into smoke. The other is a quiet, distant, steady light that can help you navigate your way home in the dark. In my youth, I chased fireworks. It took me years of getting lost to finally appreciate the stars.

This is the ultimate showdown, not between two people, but within yourself—the battle between the heart and the hormones. It's a clash that determines whether you build something that lasts or something that blows up on the launchpad.

When Lust Wears a Love Mask

. . .

Lust is a master of disguise. It feels exhilarating, all-consuming, and desperately important. It can look and sound so much like love that you'd swear it was the real thing. I should know. My first three marriages were built on the shaky ground of lust. They were whirlwinds of passion and excitement. They were also hollow.

The consequence of this confusion is that you build a life on a foundation of sand. When the tide of real-life problems comes in—and it always does—the whole structure washes away. With those early relationships, the connection was all about the good times, the thrill, the physical attraction. The moment real challenges appeared, there was nothing holding us together. The "love" we thought we had was just a mask, and underneath, we were two strangers who didn't know how to weather a storm. That disillusionment is a profound kind of heartbreak.

Spotting the Red Flags

Looking back, the red flags in those lust-driven connections were obvious, even if I chose to ignore them at the time. A relationship built on lust, not love, often shows these signs:

• **It's all about the present thrill.** The focus is on the physical connection and the immediate excitement. Conversations about the future are vague, fantastical, or avoided entirely.

• **Conflict is a dealbreaker.** Hard conversations are swept under the rug because the connection is too fragile to handle them. Real problems, financial stress, or personal struggles are seen as buzzkills, not challenges to be faced together.

• **The connection is conditional.** The affection and attention are there when things are easy and fun, but they vanish at the first sign of trouble. The ultimate red flag of a lust-based connection is a partner who disappears when the chips are down.

And then there was Molly. Our connection wasn't just a firework; it was the pilot light. When my life truly exploded—when the businesses failed and the jail doors closed—all the fireworks were long gone. But that small, steady flame of her love and commitment? It never went out. It was the one thing that kept the house from going cold and dark. That's how you know the difference. Lust runs from trouble. Love runs *toward* it.

A Chapter 4 Reflection: Examining Your Own Connections

This is the most critical distinction to make in your own life. Be honest with yourself as you consider these questions:

1 Describe a time you confused love with lust. What were the "red flags" you can now see in hindsight? What were the ultimate consequences of that confusion?

2 In your current or past relationships, what has been the "pilot light"? What are the quiet, steady, and reliable signs of connection that keep things warm, even when there are no fireworks?

3 How do you and your partner (or how have you in the past) handle conflict and crisis? Do you face it together, or does it push you apart? What does that tell you about the foundation of your relationship?

Answering these questions can be tough. It requires a level of self-awareness that many of us, myself included, have had to learn the hard way. But it's the only way to stop chasing sparks and start building a real fire.

Chapter 5: Fairy Tales and Follies

If my life were a fairy tale, the book would have been slammed shut and thrown in the fire about halfway through. The idea that love is a magical journey to a perfect "happily ever after" is, from where I'm standing, one of the most dangerous fantasies we're fed. It's a myth that sets us up for failure and disappointment, making us discard real, imperfect, and beautiful connections because they don't fit a childish script.

My life with Molly is the furthest thing from a fairy tale, and that is precisely what makes our love so strong. It wasn't bestowed by a fairy godmother; it was forged in the fires of crisis and built with the hard bricks of forgiveness and commitment.

The Myth of "Happily Ever After"

. . .

"Happily ever after" sounds like an ending, a prize you get after you find the right person. That's a folly. A real partnership doesn't have an ending until one of you is gone. It's a continuous process of choosing each other, day after day, especially on the days when it's hard.

Our "happily" wasn't found in a castle; it was found in the decision to keep going after my business collapsed. It was reaffirmed in the visiting room of a county jail then later a prison. It was rebuilt from the ashes of my failures. Happiness, in a real and lasting love, isn't a destination. It's the shelter you build together to get through the storms. Believing in a magical, effortless "ever after" is a trap that stops people from doing the hard work that real happiness requires.

Prince Charming or Just a Pumpkin?

Let me be brutally honest about my role in our story: I was no Prince Charming. For a long stretch of our life together, I was the pumpkin, waiting to be turned into something better. I was the guy who made the messes, who broke the promises, who ended up on the wrong side of the law. A woman looking for the flawless hero of a fairy tale would have—and should have—run from me at top speed.

This is the poison of the Prince Charming myth. It makes people search for perfection, for a person with no flaws, no baggage, and no history of failure. That person doesn't exist. Real love isn't about finding a perfect partner. It's about seeing the potential for a king in an imperfect man and having the strength and grace to stand by him while he figures out how to wear the crown. It's about finding someone who sees your flaws and loves you not in spite of them, but because of the person you are becoming as you overcome them.

The Damsel in Distress Has Left the Building

If I wasn't Prince Charming, then Molly was certainly no damsel in distress. The woman in those stories is helpless, passive, and waiting for a man to rescue her. That wasn't Molly. In our story, she was the one with the sword.

She wasn't waiting for a rescue; she *was* the rescue. Her strength didn't lie in her weakness, but in her incredible resilience. She was the one fighting to keep our family, our future, and our hope intact while I was busy trying to destroy it all. She rescued our life not from a dragon, but from the consequences of my own actions. The narrative of the helpless woman is an insult to the strength of real partners. A true partnership is about two people standing side-by-side, taking turns saving each other when needed.

A Chapter 5 Reflection: Rewriting Your Own Story

Breaking free from these myths requires you to become the author of your own, more realistic story. Ask yourself:

1 What "fairy tale script" are you subconsciously following

or waiting for in your own life? (e.g., waiting for a grand gesture, a "rescue," or an effortless "happily ever after.")

2 Are you searching for a "perfect" partner? What flaws in others do you see as dealbreakers that might actually just be signs of being human? What flaws in yourself are you trying to hide?

3 In what ways are you waiting to be "rescued" in your life or relationships? And in what ways can you be your own hero, or recognize the strength of a partner who is anything but a damsel in distress?

The best love stories aren't fairy tales. They are real-life epics of grit, forgiveness, and two imperfect people who refuse to give up on each other.

Chapter 6: Authenticity in the Age of Filters

∼∽∿

After you've had your failures and mistakes laid bare for the world to see, you learn a thing or two about authenticity. You learn that it's not a mask you put on to seem "real." It's what's left when all the other masks have been burned away in the fires of your own making. In an age of digital filters that smooth out every flaw, I've come to believe that true authenticity is found in the scars, not the seamless facade.

The modern world makes it easy to hide. We can filter our faces, curate our lives, and present a version of ourselves that is shinier and less complicated than the truth. But a real connection cannot be built between two avatars. It requires two real, imperfect people to have the courage to show up as they are.

The Real Deal: How to Spot Genuine Love

· · ·

In a world of performances, how do you spot the real deal? You stop listening so much to what people say, and you start watching what they do. Talk is cheap. Promises are easy to make when the sun is shining. The real test of love is consistency, especially when it's inconvenient.

I learned to spot genuine love by watching Molly. Her love wasn't in grand declarations; it was in her unwavering presence during my deepest failures. It was in her choice to stay when everyone else would have left. That's the real deal. It's not a feeling; it's a verb, an action, a commitment that shows up day after day. A partner who is only there for you when it's fun and easy is like a gym membership you only use when the weather is nice. The real measure of a partner is if they'll spot you when the weight gets heavy.

Vulnerability: The Not-So-Secret Ingredient

People talk about vulnerability as if it's a secret ingredient you can choose to sprinkle into a relationship to make it better. For me, it was never a choice. It was the main course. When you're standing in front of a judge, or when you have to tell your wife you've lost everything again, there's no room for a brave face. You are stripped bare of all pretense.

That kind of forced vulnerability is terrifying. You are showing someone the absolute worst, most broken parts of yourself. You expect them to run. But a miraculous thing can happen. When they don't run—when they look at your exposed, flawed, authentic self and stay—that's when a bond of trust is forged that is stronger than steel. It's in that moment, when you have nothing left to hide, that you create a space for a love that is truly fearless. It's radical honesty, born of necessity, and it's the only soil in which a deep connection can grow.

Beyond the Lingo: A Love That Acts

I hear people talk about "love languages" and relationship jargon, and I suppose there's some truth in it. But you have to be careful that it doesn't become another filter, another way to perform love instead of living it. It's easy to get caught up in analyzing whether someone is showing love through "acts of service" or "quality time."

What was Molly's love language? It wasn't a term from a book. Her love language was "I'm not leaving." It was an action, a simple and profound statement made not with words, but with her life. Genuine love transcends lingo. It's in the quiet support, the shared knowing glance, the hand you hold when you're scared. Let's not get so lost in the jargon that we forget to recognize the simple, powerful truth of a love that shows up.

A Chapter 6 Reflection: Finding Your Authentic Self

Authenticity starts with being honest with yourself before you can be honest with anyone else.

1 What are the "filters" you apply to your own life? What parts of yourself are you most afraid to show a partner?

· · ·

2 Think of a time you were truly vulnerable with someone. What happened? What did you learn from the experience, whether it was good or bad?

3 Beyond words, how do you *show* love and support to the people you care about? How do their actions, in turn, show their love for you?

In a world that pressures us to be perfect, the most radical act of love is to embrace our own, and our partner's, messy, beautiful, unfiltered humanity.

Chapter 7: The Road to Real

⌒∽⌒

The road from a life of fleeting connections to building something real is not a superhighway; it's a dirt track you have to clear yourself, one rock and one tree root at a time. It's a journey I know well, from the short-lived chaos of my early marriages to the 60-year partnership I've built with Molly. Understanding the difference between love and lust is the map, and authenticity is your compass. But to actually get anywhere, you have to be willing to do the work.

This is where the real journey begins. It's about making the conscious decision to stop chasing temporary thrills and start building a home for your heart.

From Flings to Things: Choosing to Build

A fling is easy. It's a rented motel room—exciting for a night, but you wouldn't want to live there. Building a real "thing"—a lasting, meaningful partnership—is like laying the foundation for a house. It's slow, unglamorous work. It requires patience, a shared vision, and the effort to dig deep, even when the ground is hard.

For Molly and me, the choice to build came after the storms had washed everything else away. We couldn't rely on the thrill of a new romance; we had to rely on a shared commitment to building a future out of the rubble of my past. This is a choice everyone has to make. You have to intentionally shift your focus from immediate gratification to long-term investment. It means filtering out connections that are only about the surface and looking for a partner who is willing to pick up a shovel and help you build, no matter what the weather looks like.

Communication Over Charades

You cannot build a house with someone by playing charades. You have to talk. You need blueprints, plans, and the ability to solve problems together. The same is true for a relationship. I see people today relying on gestures, memes, and vague cues, all while avoiding the conversations that matter.

Let me tell you, you can't play charades when you're discussing how to survive after a prison sentence. You have to use your words. You have to be brutally honest about your fears, your failures, and your hopes. Molly and I had to have conversations that were terrifyingly real. That kind of communication forges intimacy that a thousand flirty texts could never replicate.

. . .

Real communication isn't about tiptoeing around the truth to avoid a fight. It's about trusting your partner enough to tackle the truth together. It's the glue that holds everything else together. Without it, you're not partners; you're just two people guessing what the other one is thinking.

Finding Your Tribe, Even If It's a Tribe of One

People talk about the importance of "finding your tribe." In my darkest hours, my tribe had a population of one: Molly. She was my community. She was the one who showed up. This taught me that the strength of your support system isn't in its size, but in its loyalty.

Finding your tribe, whether it's one person or a dozen, isn't about finding people with the same hobbies. It's about finding people who share your core values—values like commitment, resilience, and unconditional support. These are the people who see you at your worst and don't flinch. They are the ones who form the bedrock of a truly rich and authentic life. In a world full of fake connections, a single, genuine alliance is worth more than a thousand superficial friends. Look for the people who aren't just there for the party, but who will help you clean up after the house burns down.

A Chapter 7 Reflection: Starting the Work

Building something real starts with small, intentional actions:
   1 What is one concrete step you can take *today* to invest

in a real connection, whether it's with a partner, a friend, or a family member?

2 What difficult but necessary conversation have you been avoiding? What is your fear, and what would be the first step in broaching the subject?

3 Who is in your "tribe"? Who has proven, through their actions, that they are there for you unconditionally? Take a moment to acknowledge what that support means to you.

The road to real is built not with grand gestures, but with the courage of a thousand small, honest, and consistent steps.

Chapter 8: Embracing Imperfection

Our world is obsessed with perfection—the perfect body, the perfect career, the perfect relationship displayed in a perfect Instagram post. It's a fool's errand that leaves everyone feeling inadequate. I should know. My life has been a masterclass in imperfection. And through it all, I've learned that the most beautiful things in this world are not those that are flawless, but those that have survived being broken.

Embracing imperfection is perhaps the most difficult and most important part of the journey to real love. It's where the fantasy of perfection dies and the beauty of reality begins.

The Beauty in the Breaks

For years, I tried to hide my flaws. I projected an image of a successful entrepreneur, a man who had it all under control, even as my life was spiraling. That attempt to maintain a perfect facade is what led to my biggest mistakes and my deepest pain. It was only when my imperfections were laid bare for the world to see—when my failures were undeniable—that I could finally start to build an honest life.

There's a Japanese art form called Kintsugi, where broken pottery is repaired with lacquer mixed with powdered gold. The idea is that by embracing the flaws and breaks, you make the object more beautiful and valuable than it was before. The cracks become a celebrated part of its history. My marriage to Molly is a work of Kintsugi. The breaks—my failures, my time in jail—are part of our story. They are not things to be hidden. Our love is the gold that holds the pieces together, and it is more beautiful for having been broken and repaired.

Loving the Whole Person

It's one thing to learn to accept your own flaws. It's a much greater challenge to truly accept your partner's. It's easy to love the parts of a person that are shiny and admirable. It takes real love to embrace the parts that are difficult, messy, and broken.

I gave Molly every reason to see me as nothing more than the sum of my mistakes. She could have defined me by my worst moments, and no one would have blamed her. But she never did. She saw the whole person. She knew my potential and my goodness even when I was buried under a mountain of my own bad choices.

· · ·

This is the ultimate act of love: to see someone's imperfections clearly and choose to love them anyway. It's to understand that their scars are part of their story, just as yours are part of yours. It's a love that doesn't demand perfection because it knows that our flaws are what make us human, and overcoming them together is what makes a partnership divine.

A Chapter 8 Reflection: Finding the Gold in the Cracks

Learning to embrace imperfection is a practice, not a destination. It starts with compassion for yourself and for others.

1 What imperfections in yourself are you struggling to accept? How could you begin to see them not as sources of shame, but as part of the Kintsugi of your own life story?

2 Think of a person you love. What is one of their "flaws" that you can choose to embrace with more compassion? How does that imperfection contribute to who they are as a whole person?

3 How can you create a "safe harbor" in your relationships where both you and your partner feel comfortable being imperfect? What would that look and feel like?

When you stop chasing the illusion of perfection, you open yourself up to the profound, resilient, and honest beauty of a love that is real.

Chapter 9: Conclusion: The only Takeaway That Matters

We started this journey talking about my 60-year marriage, and it's only fitting that we end there. I've spent this book exploring the landscape of what I call "fake love"—the superficial connections, the confusing sparks of lust, the impossible fairy-tale standards. But looking back at these pages, I realize I wasn't really writing about fake love at all. I was writing a thank you note to a real one.

Everything I've learned about the difference between a fragile connection and a lasting one, I learned from my life with Molly. It's a lesson that was forged in failure and sealed by forgiveness. If there is one single takeaway from my story, from this entire book, it is this: Real love is not something you find in a state of perfection. It's something you build in a state of imperfection.

It's not a firework; it's the pilot light that keeps the house warm through the winter of your failures.

· · ·

It's not a fairy tale; it's the gritty, real-life epic you write together, full of monsters you have to face as a team.

It's not a flawless diamond; it's the beautiful, golden repair of Kintsugi, where the cracks become the most valuable part of the story.

The journey to that kind of love requires you to stop chasing shiny objects and start doing the work. It demands that you trade your fear of vulnerability for the strength of authenticity. And most of all, it asks you to believe that you, and the partner you choose, are worthy of love not in spite of your flaws, but because of the grace and courage you show in embracing them.

So, what is the future of relationships? I have no idea. But I know that the fundamental truth of human connection does not change. In any era, in any landscape, the principles are the same.

Choose honesty over performance.

Choose commitment over convenience.

Choose a partner who chooses you, especially when you are at your worst.

In the end, my advice is simple. Forget about finding the perfect person who will make your life a fairy tale. Instead, find someone who will help you clean up after the house burns down. Then, spend the rest of your life building a new one together, brick by honest brick.

To Molly, whose ordinary days have always been extraordinary to me.

The Awkward First Date

The Art of Ordering the Right Drink

Ordering the right drink can feel like an art form, one that requires finesse, confidence, and just the right amount of bravado. Picture this: you're at a romantic bar, the mood is perfect, and you're ready to impress. You glance at the drink menu like it's a complex piece of modern art. Suddenly, the bartender's waiting for you to make a decision, and there you are, frozen like a deer in headlights, pondering whether a "Mojito" or "Martini" will really convey your undying love better. Spoiler alert: it won't. But fear not, dear reader, for we're here to navigate this treacherous terrain together.

First things first, let's talk about the classics. A Martini may scream sophistication, but it can also whisper "I have commitment issues." You don't want to send mixed signals while ordering. If you choose a drink that requires a twenty-step preparation and the bartender to wear a top hat, what does that say about you? It might suggest you're either a hopeless romantic or someone who's just trying too hard. Instead, go for something that reflects your personality. If you're bubbly and fun, maybe a Mimosa is your spirit drink. Just make sure you don't order it at night unless you want to be the person who perpetually lives in brunch mode.

Now let's consider the trendy options. Craft cocktails are all the rage, and you want to impress your date with your knowledge of artisanal bitters and organic garnishes. But beware! Ordering something with a name like "The Smoky Pineapple Adventure" may lead to a delightful drink or a confusing concoction that tastes like a campfire. You don't want your date thinking you're adventurous if you can't even handle a drink with a hint of smoke. Stick to drinks that sound fun but won't make you feel like you're drinking a science experiment gone wrong.

And let's not forget about the non-drinkers or those who enjoy a good mocktail. In a world where love is often represented by clinking glasses filled with something bubbly, choosing a non-alcoholic option can feel like a betrayal. But ordering a fancy mocktail can also be a bold statement. It shows that you value flavor and creativity without the need for alcohol. Plus, who doesn't love a good drink that looks like it should come with a tiny umbrella? Just be prepared for the inevitable questions about your life choices. "Are you on a cleanse? Are you pregnant? Do you just really hate fun?" Just smile and say you're embracing the 'you' without the buzz.

In conclusion, remember that the drink you order is more than just a beverage; it's a reflection of who you are and how you want to be perceived. Whether you choose a classic, a trendy mix, or a mocktail, let it be a joyous expression of yourself. Approach the bar with confidence, make your selection, and enjoy the beauty of the moment. After all, love is about connection, and if you can bond over a shared taste in drinks (or a good laugh when one of you orders something utterly ridiculous), then you're already on the right path. Cheers to love, laughter, and the delightful art of ordering the right drink!

The Rollercoaster of Relationships

The Ups: Love at First Sight (or at Least First Bite)

Love at first sight is a concept as old as time itself, often portrayed in movies with sweeping music and dreamy gazes. But let's be real: love at first bite? Now that's a true romance waiting to happen. Picture this: you're at a crowded food festival, and your eyes lock onto a sumptuous, gooey slice of pizza. The cheese is melting, the pepperoni glistens, and suddenly, all those other people fade into the background. In that moment, it's just you and the pizza, and you know this is the start of a beautiful relationship.

Now, some might argue that you can't fall head over heels for a slice of pepperoni, but those people clearly haven't experienced true culinary passion. You might think it's a bit ridiculous, but let's face it—food has the magical ability to transport us to a different state of happiness. The first bite of that pizza, where the cheese stretches and the flavors explode, can evoke feelings that no rom-com ever could. It's a moment of connection that transcends mere sustenance; it's like your taste buds are singing a duet with your heart.

Of course, not every love story is as straightforward as a pizza.

Sometimes, you take a bite of something that looks promising, only to find out it's a culinary disaster. Remember that time you were convinced that sushi was going to be your soulmate, but it turned out to be a betrayal of epic proportions? One too many seaweed-wrapped surprises, and suddenly, you're questioning everything you thought you knew about love and culinary choices. But just like in actual relationships, every bite is a lesson learned, and sometimes you have to endure a few bad meals to appreciate the good ones.

The beauty of love at first bite is that it teaches us to be adventurous. You might not know what a durian is, but you're willing to try it because, hey, life's too short to stick to boring old sandwiches. Each new dish is a potential soulmate, just waiting for you to take that leap of faith. Plus, there's something hilariously romantic about sharing a plate of food with someone special, debating the merits of pineapple on pizza while trying not to let the sauce stain your shirt. It's the little moments of laughter and shared experiences that make food—and love—so unforgettable.

So, the next time you find yourself at a restaurant or food truck, remember that love can come in many forms. Whether it's a perfectly cooked steak or a soft, warm cookie, embrace the sparks that fly when you take that first bite. Love at first sight may be the stuff of dreams, but love at first bite? Now that's a flavor to savor. So go ahead, indulge in your culinary crushes, and who knows? You might just discover that the most delicious romances are found not just in the eyes, but also on your plate.

The Downs: Misunderstandings That Could Fill a Novel

In the grand romantic comedy that is life, misunderstandings often take center stage, making you wonder if love comes with a manual—or at least a comedy script. Picture this: two people are madly in love, gazing into each other's eyes at a cozy café. One partner leans in and whispers sweet nothings while the other mishears "I love your zest for life" as "I love your chest hair." Cue the awkward laughter and a sudden need for a haircut. These small yet hilarious blunders can lead to epic tales that would make even Shakespeare chuckle in his grave.

Let's not forget the classic case of the "texting misfire." You know the drill: your partner sends a message intended for you, but instead, it lands in the chat with your mother. "Can't wait to see you tonight, baby! I'll wear that outfit you like." Suddenly, your mom is left questioning your fashion choices and deciding whether it's too late to schedule a therapy session. And just when you thought your relationship was filled with romance, it turns into a family sitcom where everyone's in on the joke—except for your mom, who is now convinced you've joined a secret nudist colony.

Then there's the notorious "I thought you meant..." scenario. You ask your partner what they want for dinner, and they respond with "surprise me." You take this as an invitation to whip up your famous burnt lasagna, only to find them horrified and questioning your culinary skills. "Surprise" in this case was not the thrill of an unexpected meal but rather the horror of a kitchen disaster. The laughter that ensues might just be the glue that keeps your relationship strong—or at least the reason you both decide to order takeout next time.

Don't even get me started on the misunderstandings that arise from watching romantic films together. One partner might get swept up in the emotional whirlwind of a tear-jerker, while the other is just trying to figure out why the protagonist hasn't yet realized that love is not about grand gestures but rather about who takes out the trash. The tears flow, the popcorn flies, and by the end of the movie, you're left with a heartwarming moment where you both realize that love is about compromise—like agreeing to watch an action flick next time to avoid any more emotional roller-coasters.

In the end, these misunderstandings are the quirks of love that make relationships uniquely entertaining. They're the stories you'll share at gatherings, the moments that become your inside jokes, and the experiences that remind you that love isn't just about perfect harmony. It's about the delightful chaos that comes with two imperfect people trying to navigate life together. So, embrace the misfires, the awkward moments, and the ridiculous misunderstandings—they're all part of the beautiful mess that is love.

The Loop-de-Loops: Surviving the Crazy Ex Stories

Ah, the crazy ex stories—those rollercoaster rides that can leave you dizzy and questioning your life choices. You know, the ones that make you feel like you've just stepped off a spinning ride at the county fair, clutching your stomach and wondering how you ended up here. Everyone has at least one story that could make a great movie plot, complete with unexpected twists, dramatic music, and maybe even a talking animal for comic relief. Surviving these tales of love gone wrong is not just a rite of passage; it's practically an Olympic sport.

First up, let's talk about the ex who took "keeping in touch" to a whole new level. You know the type—one minute you're enjoying a quiet evening with a pint of ice cream, and the next, your phone lights up with a "just checking in" text at 2 a.m. This ex has a PhD in passive-aggressive messages and a black belt in "I'll be there in five minutes" surprises. You might find yourself wondering if they've secretly enrolled in a course called "How to Make Your Ex's Life a Living Hell." The best strategy here? Perfect the art of the polite but firm "I'm busy" response, while mentally drafting your future memoir titled "The Night My Ex Tried to Burn Down My New Relationship."

Then there's the ex who seems to have a sixth sense for when you're finally moving on. Just when you've perfected your new dating profile and are ready to dive back into the dating pool, this ex swoops in like a superhero with a cringe-worthy backstory. They'll send you a message that's either a nostalgic trip down memory lane or a desperate plea to rekindle the flame, complete with a montage of your best moments together. You're left wondering if they've been lurking in the shadows like a romantic ninja, just waiting for their moment to strike. Remember, folks, it's all about timing. Your best defense is a good offense: a witty come-back that will leave them reeling and questioning their life choices.

Now, let's discuss the ex who has an uncanny ability to find love in the most unexpected places. You're scrolling through social media, minding your own business, when you stumble upon their engagement announcement. You do a double take, squint at the screen, and then spill your drink all over your keyboard. How did they go from "we're just not meant to be" to planning a wedding with someone who looks like they belong in a magazine? It's almost as if they've been secretly collecting relationship points while you were busy healing your heart. The key here is to embrace the absurdity. Send them a congratulatory message that's dripping with sarcasm and a hint of genuine happiness—because the universe has a funny way of balancing things out.

Finally, we can't forget about the ex who refuses to let go of the past. They pop up at the most inconvenient moments, like a bad sequel to a movie that should have ended after the first installment. Whether it's at a mutual friend's wedding or your favorite coffee shop, they'll always find a way to remind you of the time they "accidentally" set your favorite sweater on fire. Surviving these encounters requires a solid game plan: practice your best "I'm doing great" smile while internally chanting, "This too shall pass." Remember, love is a loop-de-loop, and sometimes you just have to hold on tight and enjoy the ride, even if it makes your stomach churn.

So, here's the takeaway: surviving the crazy ex stories is all about perspective, humor, and a little bit of resilience. These expe-riences, while often cringe-worthy, are part of the colorful tapestry of love that makes life so entertaining. Embrace the chaos, share your own tales, and above all, keep your sense of humor intact. After all, love is what it is, and sometimes, it's a wild, winding ride filled with unexpected surprises that make the journey all the more memorable.

Love Languages: The Dialects of Affection

~∞~

Words of Affirmation: Sweet Nothings and Awkward Compliments

Words of affirmation can sometimes feel like a linguistic dance, a delightful waltz where the right words can sweep someone off their feet, and the wrong ones can trip them up like a clumsy giraffe on roller skates. We've all been there, trying to muster up the courage to say something sweet, only to have it tumble out awkwardly, like a cat attempting to fit into a too-small box. "You have the most beautiful smile" is great, but when it comes out as "Your teeth are really... white!" it can lead to a moment of silence that's only broken by the sound of crickets chirping.

Let's not forget the classic "sweet nothings." These are the saccharine phrases that can melt hearts faster than ice cream on a summer day. However, we must tread carefully because not all sweet nothings are created equal. Telling someone, "You make my heart race like a hamster on a wheel" might elicit giggles rather than swoons. It's all about context. The ideal sweet nothing should be like the perfect slice of cake: just the right amount of sweetness, with a sprinkle of charm, and definitely not something that makes you question the baker's sanity.

Then there are awkward compliments, which are like the surprise twist at the end of a rom-com—unexpected and sometimes cringeworthy. Picture this: you're at a party, and you spot someone looking particularly dapper. Instead of a simple "You look nice," you blurt out, "That shirt is so bright it could guide ships to shore!" While you might think you're being clever, the recipient could be left wondering if they should thank you or seek out a lighthouse for assistance. Awkward compliments can turn a potentially romantic moment into a scene straight out of a sitcom.

Finding the right balance between genuine affection and humorous awkwardness can be a challenge. The key lies in knowing your audience. If your partner appreciates a good dad joke or enjoys the occasional pun, you might hit the sweet spot with, "You're the peanut butter to my jelly—without you, I'm just a boring piece of bread!" However, if your partner is more of a romantic poet, they might roll their eyes at your sandwich analogy and wish you'd stuck to something more heartfelt. It's a fine line between endearing and bewildering, like a cat trying to hug a dog.

In the end, words of affirmation are a powerful tool in the love toolkit. They can build someone up or leave them wondering if they accidentally wandered into a comedy club instead of a romantic rendezvous. So, the next time you feel the urge to shower your beloved with sweet nothings or compliments, remember to keep it light and playful. After all, laughter is one of love's greatest companions—just make sure your jokes don't leave them searching for the nearest exit!

Acts of Service: The Dishes that Spell Romance

In the grand symphony of romance, there's an unsung hero that often goes unnoticed: the humble act of doing the dishes. Yes, you heard that right! While most people think romance is all about candlelit dinners and moonlit walks, nothing says "I love you" quite like a sparkling clean kitchen. Picture this: your partner walks in, and there you are, suds flying, singing off-key, and doing a little dance while scrubbing the pots. It's like a romantic comedy, but with less chance of winning an Oscar and more likelihood of winning a heart.

Now, you might be wondering why dishes are the secret ingredient to a successful romantic recipe. Well, let's break it down. When you take the time to wash away the remnants of last night's lasagna, you're not just cleaning; you're demonstrating love in action. It's the equivalent of writing a sonnet, except instead of paper and ink, you've got sponges and dish soap. And let's be honest, nothing says "I'm in this for the long haul" like tackling the crusty remains of dinner together. Just imagine the bonding moments as you argue over whether to soak or scrub. That's the stuff love stories are made of!

Of course, the real magic happens when you surprise your partner by tackling the dishes without being asked. It's like finding out that the pizza delivery guy also moonlights as a magician because, poof, the dishes are done and the kitchen sparkles! Your partner will look at you with a mix of disbelief and adoration, as if you've just pulled a rabbit out of a hat. "Who knew you had it in you?" they might say, and you can reply with a wry smile, "I've been practicing for this moment my entire life."

Now, let's not forget the charming debates that arise from dish duty. Who knew that a simple chore could lead to such passionate discussions? "I believe plates should be stacked this way!" versus "No, clearly it's this way!" It's as if you're reenacting a scene from a courtroom drama, complete with exaggerated gestures and a flair for the dramatic. And while you might be tempted to turn it into a full-blown argument, just remember: the goal is to clean the dishes, not to win a Pulitzer Prize for the best debate performance.

In the end, acts of service like doing the dishes are more than just chores; they're opportunities for connection and laughter. So, the next time you find yourself staring down a mountain of dirty dishes, remember that you're not just cleaning; you're crafting a romantic masterpiece. And who knows? You might even find that the best moments in your relationship are forged not in grand gestures but in those everyday acts that spell love—like washing away the remnants of dinner together, one soapy dish at a time.

Gifts: When a Coffee Mug Means "I Love You"

In the grand tapestry of romance, few gifts say "I love you" quite like a coffee mug. Sure, diamonds are forever, but have you ever tried sipping your morning brew from a diamond-encrusted mug? Spoiler alert: it's not as practical as it sounds, and you might end up with more than just a caffeine buzz. A coffee mug, on the other hand, is a daily reminder of affection. It's a vessel for warmth, comfort, and the occasional accidental spill that leads to a sweeping declaration of "I love you" from the floor when you realize your favorite mug is now an abstract art piece.

Choosing the right coffee mug can feel like a relationship itself. You start by browsing through endless options online, trying to find one that encapsulates your partner's essence. You might come across a mug that says "World's Okayest Partner" and think, "Perfect!" But then, you remember that love is not just about settling for okay. You want a mug that sparks joy, one that elicits a grin every morning, even if it's just because it features a cat wearing a sombrero. Remember, laughter is the best seasoning for love, and what better way to spice up breakfast than with a quirky mug?

The real beauty of gifting a coffee mug is in the little things. It's not just a present; it's an opportunity for connection. Picture this: you hand your beloved the mug, and they take a moment to read the silly slogan written on it. They chuckle, and in that moment, you've created a shared memory, a bond over the ridiculousness of life. Each time they sip coffee from that mug, they're not just getting their caffeine fix; they're reminded of your thoughtful gesture and the laughter it brought. It's like a daily love note that says, "Hey, remember that time you almost choked on your coffee because of my terrible joke? Good times!"

Of course, there are risks involved in gifting a coffee mug. For instance, you might accidentally choose one with a message like "I'm Not a Regular Mom, I'm a Cool Mom," which can lead to a series of eye rolls and an immediate conversation about how you should probably just stick to standard gifts like socks. But isn't that part of the fun? Love is about navigating those awkward moments together, and if your partner can laugh at the mug you so enthusiastically gifted, then they're probably a keeper. After all, what's love without a little bit of humor and the occasional cringe?

In the end, a coffee mug is more than just ceramic; it's a symbol of love, laughter, and the everyday moments that make life beautiful. So the next time you're pondering what to get your significant other, remember that a simple mug can hold more than just coffee. It can hold memories, laughter, and perhaps even a few secrets shared over steaming cups of joe. Love is what it is, and sometimes it's as simple as a warm beverage and a silly mug that says, "You're the cream in my coffee."

Communication: The Love Signal

❧

Texting: The New Love Letter

Texting has become the modern-day equivalent of the love letter, minus the wax seal and romantic candlelight. Gone are the days when you would spend hours crafting the perfect note, only to have it delivered by a friend who might drop it in the mud on the way to your crush. Now, with just a thumb, you can hit send and have your heartfelt (or hastily written) sentiments delivered in an instant. Sure, the romance of handwritten prose may have its charm, but let's be honest: nothing says "I love you" quite like a perfectly timed GIF of a cat falling off a table.

The beauty of texting is that it caters to our desire for immediacy. We no longer need to wait for the mailman to deliver our feelings; instead, we can share our innermost thoughts while standing in line at the grocery store. What's more romantic than typing "I miss you" while debating whether to buy organic or regular bananas? And let's not forget the thrill of receiving a text from that special someone. That little vibration in your pocket feels like a mini rollercoaster ride of emotions. You open it, heart racing, only to find they've sent you a meme about how they love pizza more than people. Ah, true love.

Yet, texting can also be a minefield of miscommunication. A simple "K" can send your heart plummeting into a chasm of despair. Did they mean "Okay, cool" or "Okay, I'm done with this conversation"? The ambiguity of text can turn even the most confident lover into a detective, analyzing every punctuation mark like it holds the secrets of the universe. "Why didn't they add an exclamation point? Are they mad at me? Should I send a follow-up emoji?" The possibilities are endless, and let's be real, it's enough to drive anyone a little bonkers.

And let's not overlook the art of the emoji. Those little yellow faces have transformed how we express love and affection, but they come with their own set of challenges. Do you go for the classic heart, or is that too cliché? Maybe a winking face will convey your playful nature? But heaven forbid you accidentally send a peach emoji instead of a heart, and suddenly your sweet nothings take a very different turn. Love in the age of texting requires a PhD in emoji linguistics, and even then, you might just end up in the awkward zone of misunderstanding.

In the end, texting may not replace the timeless charm of a love letter, but it certainly adds a layer of hilarity to modern romance. Whether it's misinterpreted messages or the thrill of a new notification, the digital love letter is here to stay. So embrace the chaos, laugh at the misunderstandings, and remember that love, in all its forms, is still what it is—a beautiful, messy, and often hilarious journey.

The Power of Emojis: Heart Eyes and Facepalms

In the grand theater of modern romance, emojis have taken center stage, wielding the power to convey emotions faster than you can say "I love you." Picture this: you're on a first date, and as your date tells a charming story about their cat, you send a heart eyes emoji. Suddenly, they think you're ready to adopt a feline family together! But fear not, for emoji miscommunication is the spice of dating. That heart eyes icon can express admiration, or it could just mean you're really into their dessert choice. It's a fine line between affection and dessert envy!

Now, let's talk about the infamous facepalm emoji. This little gem has the power to encapsulate our most cringeworthy moments in love. Whether it's accidentally texting your crush a meme meant for your best friend or confusing their name with your ex's, a well-placed facepalm can say "Oops, I did it again" without the need for a full-blown apology. It's a universal signal that says, "I'm human, I mess up, but here's a light-hearted way to acknowledge it." In a world where we all want to appear polished, the facepalm is a refreshing reminder that we're all just a little bit ridiculous.

Then there's the joy of using emojis to spice up those mundane love notes. Sending a simple "Thinking of you" can easily be transformed into an epic love declaration with the right combination of emojis. A heart, a slice of pizza, and a dancing cat can convey that you think of your partner as the ideal companion for both romance and late-night snacks. Who wouldn't want to be the subject of such culinary affection? Suddenly, love notes become a cryptic puzzle that requires a decoder ring. "What does the taco mean?" you might ask, only to realize it symbolizes your taco Tuesday tradition. Nothing says love like food!

Of course, emojis can also help you navigate the treacherous waters of dating. Imagine receiving a text that reads, "I had a great time last night 😊 " versus "I had a great time last night." The former gives you butterflies and makes you feel like you're starring in a rom-com, while the latter feels like a polite nod from an acquaintance. The right emoji can transform a simple message into a heartfelt declaration, turning an everyday conversation into a page from a love story. It's like giving your words a makeover, complete with a sparkling new outfit and a dash of charisma!

Finally, we must acknowledge that with great power comes great responsibility. With the emoji palette at our fingertips, it's easy to misfire. So before you send that wink emoji to your significant other, pause for a moment and think, "Am I trying to flirt or just acknowledging how cute their new haircut is?" The line between romantic interest and friendly banter can be as thin as a strand of spaghetti. In the end, emojis are the delightful, chaotic, and sometimes confusing symbols of love in the digital age. Embrace the heart eyes and facepalms, for they are the laughter and joy woven into the tapestry of our romantic adventures!

The Joy of Miscommunication: When "What's for Dinner?" Becomes a Debate

In relationships, the simple question "What's for dinner?" can quickly escalate into a full-blown debate worthy of the most heated political forums. It starts innocently enough, with one partner innocently looking for a meal to satisfy their hunger. But as soon as the words leave their lips, it's as if they've thrown a match onto a pile of dry leaves. Suddenly, dinner is no longer just a meal; it becomes a battleground of preferences, dietary restrictions, and culinary aspirations. The room fills with the tension of unspoken expectations and the faint sound of a clock ticking down to an inevitable showdown.

The first miscommunication often arises from the sheer vagueness of the question itself. One partner might be thinking of a gourmet three-course meal, while the other is dreaming of a quick bowl of cereal. It's like asking a toddler what they want to do today —good luck getting a straight answer! You may end up with a request for "something delicious" that could range from sushi to a peanut butter sandwich. As each partner tries to navigate the minefield of choices, simple dinner plans morph into a whimsical guessing game. It's a comedy of errors where one person's "spaghetti" is another's "vegan gluten-free noodle surprise," leading to confusion and, of course, laughter.

Then comes the inevitable blame game. If one partner suggests tacos and the other admits to hating them, you can hear the collective sigh of disappointment echoing through the house. "How could you not like tacos?" becomes a rhetorical question loaded with the weight of unmet expectations. Suddenly, dinner has morphed into a reflection of personal values and past traumas—because let's face it, who knew that a simple meal could unveil the intricacies of one's childhood experiences with food? The joy of miscommunication shines through as couples realize they're not just negotiating a meal; they're navigating a complex web of emotions and preferences that they never even knew existed.

As the clock ticks closer to dinner time, the stakes get higher. Each suggestion feels like a risk, and soon both partners find themselves in a culinary stand-off reminiscent of a classic Western stand-off. "I could make a mean stir-fry," one might suggest, while the other rolls their eyes as if the very idea is an affront to their palate. At this point, it's less about dinner and more about pride. The laughter bubbles up as they realize they're debating like politicians, except the stakes involve not only their dinner plans but also the prospect of an evening filled with takeout menus and fridge raids.

Ultimately, the joy of miscommunication in the realm of meal planning serves as a reminder that love is not just about romance and shared dreams. It's also about the humorous, sometimes absurd moments that arise from the everyday. Every debate over dinner is a chance to learn about each other, to embrace quirks, and to laugh at the chaos of life together. In the end, whether it's tacos, stir-fry, or cereal, it doesn't matter as long as there's love, laughter, and perhaps a little takeout on the table. After all, isn't that what love is all about?

The Family Factor

Meeting the Parents: A Comedy of Errors

Meeting the parents can feel like stepping onto a stage where the stakes are high, and the script is entirely improvised. As the day approached, I couldn't help but imagine my partner's family as a quirky sitcom cast, complete with oddball characters and laugh tracks. I envisioned the father as a gruff but lovable figure, the mother as the ultimate homemaker, and maybe even a sibling who would keep throwing in snarky one-liners. I felt like I was preparing for an audition, and I was determined to steal the show. Little did I know, I was about to become the comic relief.

The day finally arrived, and I rolled up to their house with a bouquet of flowers that looked like they had been through a windstorm. I confidently knocked on the door, only for it to swing open to reveal my partner's younger sibling, who was dressed like they had just walked out of a video game. After a moment of silence, they burst into laughter, pointing at my wilted bouquet. I tried to play it cool, claiming it was an avant-garde statement on the fleeting nature of love, but I could feel my face heating up like a toaster. The sibling's chuckles echoed in my ears as I stepped inside, already regretting my choice of gift.

As I settled into the living room, I quickly realized that the family dynamic was like an elaborate game of charades. My partner's father cracked jokes that flew over my head, while the mother seamlessly transitioned from discussing her favorite hobbies to asking me about my life goals, all without a breath in between. I felt like I was undergoing a verbal obstacle course, dodging questions and trying to keep my cool as I spilled my half-baked ideas about starting a podcast. Who knew that discussing my love for obscure 80s bands could lead to such an intense interrogation about my future?

The pinnacle of my comedic misadventures came when dinner was served. The table was beautifully set, and I was both in awe and terrified. As I reached for what I thought was a bread roll, I accidentally sent a bowl of mashed potatoes flying across the room. Time seemed to slow down as I watched the creamy mass splatter against the wall, creating what could only be described as a modern art masterpiece. The room erupted in laughter, and instead of feeling mortified, I joined in. After all, who couldn't appreciate a little culinary chaos? If anything, I was now part of the family story, the "potato incident" that would be retold at gatherings for years to come.

By the end of the evening, I had survived the gauntlet of parental scrutiny and emerged with a newfound appreciation for the unpredictability of love. Meeting the parents was less about impressing them with my charm and more about embracing the hilarity of the situation. As I left, I could hear the family still chuckling about my mashed potato disaster. It was a reminder that love isn't just about the perfect moments; it's also about the perfectly imperfect ones. And just like that, I realized that in the grand comedy of love, sometimes the best scenes are the ones that go completely off-script.

Family Gatherings: Love or Hostage Situation?

Family gatherings: the events that promise laughter, food, and a healthy dose of chaos. It's a delightful paradox where love meets the reality of long-lost relatives asking if you've found a job yet or when you'll finally settle down. The air is thick with the smell of Grandma's famous casserole, and the tension might be just as palpable as the aroma. You can practically hear the collective sighs of family members as they brace themselves for the inevitable questions that feel more like an inquisition than a casual chat. Love may be in the air, but so is the smell of Aunt Edna's tuna salad that no one asked for.

Picture this: you walk into a room filled with family members who haven't seen you since the last holiday gathering, and suddenly, you're the star of a reality show called "Guess What You're Doing Wrong with Your Life." Cousins who once played tag in the backyard now seem to have PhDs in unsolicited advice. The pressure to explain your life choices can turn a simple "How have you been?" into a multi-act play of justifications. Who knew that loving your job as a barista could evoke such deep concern? "But honey, you can't live on coffee alone!" they say, oblivious to the fact that you do, indeed, survive on coffee and dreams.

Then there's the charming tradition of family games. Nothing says "we love each other" quite like a heated game of charades where Uncle Bob insists on using interpretive dance to convey "The Godfather." Watching him flail around while everyone else tries to guess is a comedy goldmine, but it's also a reminder of how family gatherings can morph into a competitive sport. The stakes are high, and suddenly you're rooting for your team while trying to avoid the awkward eye contact with Grandma, who is convinced that your team has a distinct advantage—mostly because you're younger and, in her eyes, inherently more clever.

Let's not forget the heartwarming yet utterly exhausting tradition of group photos. The moment the camera clicks, you can almost hear the collective groan as everyone attempts to strike a pose that says, "We're the perfect family" while simultaneously thinking, "Please don't post this on social media." The kids are crying, the dog has run off with the neighbor's sandwich, and someone's wearing a sweater that could only be described as a crime against fashion. Yet, in the midst of this chaotic scene, you can't help but feel a warm glow of affection. You're all in this together, facing the absurdity of life with a shared bond that somehow makes it all worthwhile.

In the end, family gatherings are a delightful mix of love and hostage situation vibes. You might leave with a headache from the noise and an eye twitch from the questions, but you'll also carry with you the laughter, the memories, and maybe even a few leftover slices of pie. Love is indeed what it is—messy, hilarious, and often overwhelming—but it's those very moments that remind us of what family is all about. So, the next time you find yourself at a family gathering, embrace the chaos. After all, it's all part of the beautiful, bizarre tapestry of love that binds us together.

Sibling Rivalry: Can Love Really Conquer All?

Sibling rivalry is like the ultimate reality show that runs in every household, complete with plot twists, dramatic confrontations, and surprise alliances. You've got your classic scenarios: the battle for the last piece of pizza, the eternal debate over who gets the biggest slice of cake, or the well-timed snatch of a toy just as the other sibling is about to reach for it. It's a competition that never truly ends, even when the siblings grow up and are supposed to be "mature." Spoiler alert: maturity is overrated, especially when there's a chance to throw shade at your brother's questionable haircut from 1995.

As the years roll on, these sibling rivalries transform into a sort of comedic routine. You've got your two main characters—the overachiever and the underachiever. The overachiever is usually the one who can do no wrong, with a resume that reads like a super-hero's biography, while the underachiever is perfecting the art of procrastination, often with a bag of chips in one hand and the TV remote in the other. Yet, amid this chaotic comedy, there's a question that looms large: can love really conquer all, or is it just a clever tagline for a rom-com?

The truth is, love gets put to the test more often than an awkward family gathering. Picture this: the overachiever finally invites the underachiever to a fancy dinner party, and the underachiever shows up in sweatpants, ready to raid the snack table. Cue the eye rolls and the whispered critiques. But deep down, there's an unspoken bond that often shines through the chaos. Love is that invisible force that somehow allows the overachiever to look past the sweatpants and the chips and still hope for a decent conversation. It's the subtle acknowledgment that, no matter how many competitive jabs are thrown, they are still family.

Sibling rivalry can sometimes morph into that unique blend of love and annoyance, where the love is always there but often buried under layers of teasing and playful insults. It's the kind of love that can survive a thousand eye rolls and a million sarcastic comments. The bond is fortified through shared childhood memories of teaming up against the parents, and those ridiculous inside jokes that no one else gets. In many ways, it's like a rollercoaster ride— thrilling and nauseating all at once, but absolutely unforgettable.

In the end, the question remains: can love indeed conquer all? Well, if love can survive the countless battles over who gets to sit in the front seat during family road trips, or who can claim the TV remote during family movie night, then yes, love can conquer sibling rivalry. It may not mean that the rivalry will ever completely vanish, but love will ensure that there's always a safety net ready to catch the falling comedies of life, proving that even in the most intense sibling rivalries, love is what it is—messy, chaotic, but oh-so-necessary.

The Friends' Influence

The Wingman: Your Best Friend or Your Worst Enemy?

The wingman: a title that carries more weight than the average person might realize. One minute, they're helping you score that dreamy date at the bar; the next, you're left wondering if they're secretly trying to sabotage your love life for their own amusement. Let's face it, the role of the wingman can be as slippery as a banana peel on a dance floor. You think they've got your back, but there's always that chance they'll trip you up instead, just for kicks.

Picture this: you're at a party, heart racing, and you spot the perfect potential partner across the room. You summon your courage and prepare to make your move. Enter the wingman, who's supposed to swoop in with suave confidence and distract the competition. Instead, they start an impromptu karaoke session, belting out off-key 80s hits, drawing all attention away from you. You're standing there, contemplating if it's possible to disappear into thin air while your wingman is living their best life, completely oblivious to your internal crisis.

Now, let's not forget the infamous "helpful advice" that wingmen love to dispense. Just when you think you're about to impress someone with your dazzling wit, your wingman jumps in with their own version of charm. "Oh, you like hiking? My friend here has climbed Mount Everest—twice!" Suddenly, you're in a competition you didn't sign up for, and your wingman is playing the role of the overzealous hype man. You're left wondering if they're really trying to help or if they just enjoy watching you sweat.

Of course, not all wingman experiences are disastrous. Sometimes, they're the unsung heroes of your love life, swooping in with the perfect icebreaker or a hilarious anecdote that makes you look like a total catch. They can help you navigate the treacherous waters of awkward small talk and even give you that much-needed pep talk when you're feeling like a romantic disaster. A good wingman knows when to step back and let you shine, like a supportive sidekick in a rom-com, but only if they don't get too carried away with their own antics first.

In the end, the true test of a wingman lies in their ability to make you laugh at the absurdity of it all. Whether they're your best friend or your worst enemy, having someone by your side during the wild ride of dating can turn a potential disaster into a memorable adventure. So, the next time you're gearing up for a night out with your wingman, remember to brace yourself for anything and everything. After all, love is what it is, and sometimes it's a comedy of errors with a side of friendship.

Friends vs. Lovers: The Ultimate Showdown

When it comes to the age-old debate of friends versus lovers, it's a bit like comparing apples and oranges—if those apples were occasionally bruised and the oranges could sometimes throw a tantrum. Friends are the ones who help you move your couch, while lovers are the ones who help you move on after that couch-related existential crisis. Friends provide the comfort of knowing that your secrets are safe, while lovers? Well, they might just turn those secrets into the plot of a romantic comedy that no one asked for.

Imagine a friend who knows you so well that they can finish your sentences. This is great until you realize they also know that your favorite late-night snack is a questionable combination of pickles and peanut butter. Enter the lover, who is charming enough to not judge your midnight cravings but just intrusive enough to suggest you try something fancier, like avocado toast—because clearly, they want to change the world one meal at a time. The friends are there for the "I can't believe they said that!" moments, while lovers are there for the "I can't believe I said that!" moments, creating a delightful cocktail of shared embarrassment.

But what happens when your best friend starts to look a little too much like a romantic interest? Suddenly, the comfortable banter transforms into a high-stakes game of emotional dodgeball. You're dodging the terrifying thought of ruining the friendship while also trying to catch those butterflies that seem to have taken up residence in your stomach. Spoiler alert: this is where the real confusion begins. Friends are safe harbors in the stormy seas of love, but lovers? They're the wild waves that might just sweep you off your feet—if you can survive the riptide of awkwardness first.

Let's not forget the classic "friend zone" dilemma. It's a place so notorious that it deserves its own zip code. Friends may offer you sage advice on how to navigate your feelings, but they also know that if you ever used the term "friend zone" in their presence, they might just roll their eyes so hard they see their brain. Lovers, however, are often the ones who capitalize on that awkwardness, throwing around phrases like "we need to talk" as if they're auditioning for a soap opera. The dramatic tension can be palpable, leading to moments that make you wonder if you should have just stuck to Netflix and ice cream with your friends.

In the end, friends and lovers have their own unique charm, like chocolate and vanilla ice cream. You may love one flavor, but sometimes a scoop of both is necessary to satisfy your cravings. Friends offer a safety net, while lovers throw you into the circus of romance, complete with clowns and cotton candy. So, whether you find yourself laughing with friends or swooning with lovers, just remember that love, in all its forms, continues to be the ultimate showdown—one that brings both laughter and a few bumps and bruises along the way.

Advice from Friends: The Good, the Bad, and the Hilarious

When it comes to love, friends can be the most entertaining and, at times, bewildering source of advice. They come armed with their own experiences, which can range from the absolutely brilliant to the downright absurd. Picture this: your best buddy, fresh off a breakup, proclaims that the key to moving on is to "date someone who looks like your ex but is definitely taller and has a dog." While the logic may be questionable, you can't help but chuckle at the absurdity of it all. Friends have a unique way of turning heartbreak into a comedy show, making you laugh even when you feel like crying.

Then there are those moments when the advice transcends ridiculousness and veers straight into the realm of the downright unhelpful. Your well-meaning friend who's never been in a serious relationship might suggest that all you need is to "just relax and be yourself." Sure, because nothing says romance quite like showing up on a date wearing pajamas and discussing your favorite Netflix series. It's these gems of wisdom that remind us that sometimes, it's best to take advice with a grain of salt—or perhaps an entire salt shaker—especially when it comes from someone whose idea of commitment is keeping a houseplant alive for more than a week.

Of course, not all advice is created equal, and there are those rare moments when your friends hit the nail on the head. These nuggets of wisdom often come wrapped in humor, like when your friend says, "If you want to keep the spark alive, just remember to never stop flirting. Even if it's just with the pizza delivery guy." This kind of playful banter serves as a reminder that love should be fun and lighthearted. It's the kind of advice that makes you realize that in the grand scheme of things, laughter can be just as important as romance itself.

Let's not forget the circus of group chats where love advice flows like a bottomless cup of coffee. One minute, you're discussing your feelings, and the next, your friends are sending memes that perfectly capture the chaos of dating. "When you finally meet the one, but they have bad taste in music" paired with a GIF of someone dramatically fainting is the kind of relatable humor that makes love seem a little less daunting. These moments highlight that while love can be complicated, it's also filled with shared experiences that are often best laughed at together.

In the end, the beauty of seeking advice from friends lies in the blend of the good, the bad, and the hilariously absurd. Each piece of advice, no matter how ridiculous, adds to the tapestry of your love life. So the next time you find yourself in a sticky romantic situation, remember to call up your friends, share a laugh, and embrace the chaos. After all, love is what it is, and sometimes, it's best approached with a hearty dose of humor and a willingness to take things less seriously.

The Mundane Moments

Grocery Shopping: The Ultimate Love Test

Grocery shopping is often considered a mundane chore, but let's be honest—it's the ultimate love test. Forget about candlelit dinners and romantic getaways; the real measure of your relationship can be found in the dairy aisle. Picture this: you and your partner stroll into the store, hand in hand, ready to tackle the week's meals. But just a few moments later, you're both staring at a wall of cereal boxes like you're deciphering hieroglyphics. This is where the love begins to show cracks or, if you're lucky, flourishes like a well-watered houseplant.

As you navigate through the aisles, the first test of love emerges: the cart. Is it a two-person operation, or does one person take over while the other pretends to read the ingredients on the back of a snack? If your partner starts pushing the cart like it's a sports car and you're in the passenger seat, it's time for a reality check. Love is all about teamwork, and in the grocery store, that means equally sharing the burden of the cart's weight, not turning it into a bumper car experience. If you can survive the cart chaos together, you just might be able to face anything life throws your way.

Next up: the produce section. Here, love is tested in the form of fruit selection. You pick up a perfectly ripe avocado, only to have your partner declare that it's "too squishy." This is where negotiations begin. Do you abandon your quest for the perfect guacamole, or do you stand your ground like a knight defending a castle? The produce section can quickly become a battlefield of opinions, but if you can reach a compromise between the "squishy avocado" and "the rock-hard one," you're destined for culinary greatness. After all, who doesn't love a good guacamole debate?

As you make your way to the checkout line, the final love test looms: the impulse buys. Will you be able to resist the siren call of the chocolate bars or the latest trendy snack? This is where trust and shared values come into play. If your partner throws a six-pack of soda into the cart while you're trying to stick to a healthy diet, a silent war can erupt. But if you both can laugh off the temptation and agree that maybe the overpriced artisanal chips can wait until next week, your bond will only strengthen. After all, love is about making choices together, and sometimes those choices include saying no to overpriced snacks.

Finally, as you leave the store with your loot, take a moment to appreciate the absurdity of it all. Grocery shopping isn't just about buying food; it's about navigating the relationship minefield, complete with cart collisions and heated debates over snack selections. It's about finding joy in the little things, like the shared laughter when you both realize you forgot the milk again. So, the next time you gear up for a grocery run, remember that it's not just a shopping trip; it's a love expedition. And if you can survive it together, there's no doubt that your love is as nourishing as the meals you'll prepare.

Netflix Decisions: Choosing a Show Without a Fight

Netflix, the modern-day oracle of entertainment, offers us an endless scroll of options that can feel more overwhelming than choosing a partner. You and your significant other settle down for a cozy night in, armed with popcorn and a blanket, only to find yourselves engaged in an epic showdown over what to watch. The battle lines are drawn: one wants a heartwarming rom-com, while the other is set on a gritty documentary about the history of shoelaces. Ah, the joys of love and Netflix!

First, let's talk about the infamous "I don't care, you choose" line. This phrase is a classic trap, akin to saying, "I love all your friends equally." It sounds great on the surface, but deep down, it's a ticking time bomb. The moment you pick a show that doesn't meet the unspoken criteria of your partner's secret wishlist, you're suddenly the villain of the evening. You'll hear a dramatic sigh that could rival any Shakespearean monologue. The trick is to pretend you care about the latest true-crime series while secretly hoping for a light-hearted adventure.

Next comes the dreaded scrolling phase, where you both swipe through titles as if you're trying to find the perfect avocado at the grocery store. "How about this one?" you ask, only to be met with a dubious eyebrow raise. You quickly realize that selecting a show is less about the actual content and more about navigating the minefield of your partner's preferences. Remember, it's not just about finding something to watch; it's about keeping the peace. So, brace yourself for the ultimate compromise: something that's half romantic, half thrilling, and definitely has at least one talking animal.

If you're still not on the same page after all this, it may be time to employ the classic "rock-paper-scissors" technique. It's simple, fair, and a little ridiculous—much like love itself. You could argue that it's a time-honored method of decision-making that has survived the test of time, much like your relationship. However, be wary; if one of you is a sore loser, this could devolve into a full-blown debate about the unfairness of life, love, and the algorithmic injustice of Netflix.

Finally, once you've reached a consensus—perhaps after a few rounds of negotiation and maybe even a snack break—there's that moment of joy when you finally press play. You snuggle in, ready to enjoy your selected masterpiece, only to find out that it's the same show you watched last week. But hey, at least you're together, right? In the grand scheme of love, it's those little moments of compromise and laughter that count. And who knows? Maybe the next time you sit down for a Netflix decision, you'll both just agree to watch whatever is trending, and save the bickering for the next dinner party.

Weekend Chores: Love is in the Dust Bunnies

When it comes to love, we often envision candlelit dinners and romantic getaways, but let's be real: most of us spend the majority of our weekends elbow-deep in the less glamorous side of life— chores. Yes, the very act of scrubbing toilets and vacuuming dust bunnies can be a surprisingly effective love language. After all, nothing says "I love you" quite like removing the evidence of last week's popcorn binge from the couch cushions.

Picture this: it's Saturday morning, and the sun is shining. You and your partner have the whole day ahead of you. Instead of diving into a Netflix marathon, you decide to tackle the mountain of laundry that's been threatening to avalanche onto the floor. As you sort colors from whites, you can't help but chuckle at how your relationship has evolved. Remember when you used to spend weekends dreaming about your future? Now, you're dreaming about the day you'll find the bottom of the laundry basket.

As you fold those shirts, you start to reminisce about the first time you saw each other in a laundry room, both awkwardly trying to impress the other with your choice of fabric softener. Who knew that detergent could be such a turn-on? Fast forward to now, and you're both arguing about the merits of hot versus cold washes. The laundry may feel like a mundane chore, but it's also a bonding experience. Each argument and shared laugh over sock mismatches is a thread weaving you closer together, even if it occasionally unravels into a sock war.

Then there's the ever-popular chore of vacuuming, where the real magic happens. Is there anything more romantic than watching your partner skillfully maneuver the vacuum cleaner, dodging furniture like a ninja while simultaneously trying to avoid getting stuck on the carpet? You can't help but giggle as they attempt to assert their dominance over the dust bunnies that have clearly formed a small army in the corner. This is a real-life battle of love against grime, and you're both on the frontline, armed with a vacuum and a sense of humor.

By the end of your weekend chore marathon, you may be covered in dust, but you're also covered in love—sticky and slightly disheveled but undeniably closer than when you started. The magic lies not just in the completion of each task, but in the shared laughter, the playful banter, and the teamwork. So, the next time you're contemplating how to spend your weekend, remember: love is indeed in the dust bunnies, and sometimes the most romantic moments are found in the least expected places, like the laundry room or the vacuum closet.

Love in the Digital Age

Dating Apps: Swiping Right on Life

In the digital age, dating apps have transformed the romantic landscape into a virtual buffet of potential partners. Picture yourself at a buffet: there's a little something for everyone, but you also need to navigate the occasional mystery meat. Swiping right has become an art form, with users deftly flicking their fingers across screens, judging suitability based on a few curated images and a catchy tagline. Who knew that a well-placed avocado toast photo could be the key to someone's heart? However, let's not forget that behind every profile lies a person, and sometimes that person is just as confusing as a riddle wrapped in an enigma.

The beauty of dating apps lies in their ability to connect people from all walks of life, but the process can feel like a game show where you're both contestant and host. How many times have you sat there, swiping through profiles, wondering if you should pick the one with the dog, the one with the mysterious quote about adventure, or the one who just seems to have a perpetual vacation tan? It's like trying to choose the best flavor of ice cream when you know you're lactose intolerant. The pressure is real, and let's be honest, sometimes you just want to swipe right on the entire lineup and hope for the best.

Of course, with great power comes great responsibility. The responsibility of crafting the perfect profile that balances charm and intrigue without sounding like a human ad for a used car. "I enjoy long walks on the beach" is a classic, but let's be real: who wants to walk when you can just lounge with a drink in hand? Navigating conversations can be even trickier, as you try to decipher whether the other person is a genuine match or just a master of small talk with a penchant for emojis. Remember, it's not about how many times you can use "LOL" in one conversation; it's about finding someone who can make you chuckle in real life.

As you dive deeper into this pixelated romance, prepare yourself for the inevitable "ghosting" phenomenon. One moment, you're sharing existential musings about the meaning of life, and the next, you're left wondering if they've been abducted by aliens. Ghosting is the dating app equivalent of being left on read, and it's more common than finding a decent avocado at the grocery store. It's enough to make anyone question whether love is truly what it is or just a series of unfortunate events played out on a smartphone screen.

Despite the quirks and challenges, dating apps offer the possibility of finding a connection that transcends the virtual world. They provide a platform for meeting individuals you might never cross paths with otherwise—like that one guy who collects vintage typewriters or the woman who has a passion for competitive cheese rolling. Love, in all its unpredictable forms, often arrives when you least expect it. So, as you swipe right on life, remember to keep an open mind, a sense of humor, and perhaps a backup plan for when things get a little too cheesy.

Social Media: Sharing Love or Oversharing?

Social media has transformed the way we express love, turning romantic gestures into public spectacles. Gone are the days of sweet handwritten notes and intimate dinners; now, love is just a hashtag away. You can declare your affection with a perfectly filtered photo captioned "My forever" or a video of your partner trying to cook dinner (which is really just an elaborate way to say, "Look how cute they are when they set the kitchen on fire"). But with this newfound public display of affection comes the question: are we sharing love, or are we just oversharing?

Let's take a moment to consider the fine line between sharing love and oversharing. There's a sweet spot where your love story can inspire others—a cute couple dancing in their living room, a lovely anniversary post, or even a heartfelt message about how your partner makes you better. But then there's the other side, where things get a bit cringeworthy. You know, the couple that posts daily updates on their breakfast choices together or the ones who feel the need to document every single fight and makeup session. I mean, who really wants to know about the time you had an argument over who left the toilet seat up? Spoiler alert: nobody!

Let's not forget those couples who have taken it to the extreme with relationship goals. You know those perfectly curated feeds that look like they just stepped out of a romance movie? The couple frolicking on a beach at sunset, followed by a post about how they "just can't live without each other." Meanwhile, in reality, one of them is probably hiding behind the camera, rolling their eyes at the whole charade. The truth is, love isn't always picture-perfect; sometimes it's messy, chaotic, and full of inside jokes that no one else would understand. So why not embrace the glorious messiness of love instead of trying to fit it into a social media box?

And let's not overlook the unsolicited advice that comes with sharing love online. Post a picture of you and your partner on a hike, and suddenly you're bombarded with comments like, "You should get married!" or "When are the babies coming?" It's as if people forget that love is about the journey, not the destination. Maybe the couple just wanted to enjoy a peaceful walk without a side of pressure! It's a fine balance between sharing joy and inviting the world to weigh in on your relationship decisions. Sometimes, it feels less like a celebration of love and more like a social media version of "The Hunger Games"—may the odds be ever in your favor!

In the end, social media can be a wonderful tool for sharing love, but it's essential to navigate it with a sense of humor and a healthy dose of self-awareness. While it's tempting to showcase every sweet moment, remember that love thrives in the genuine and the imperfect. So, go ahead and post that adorable picture of you both, but maybe leave out the details of your latest spat over laundry. After all, love is meant to be shared, but not in a way that turns your relationship into a reality show. Embrace the joy, the laughter, and even the chaos—because love, in all its forms, is what it is.

Virtual Love: When Your Heart is Just a Click Away

In the age of technology, love has taken on a whole new form, and it's often just a click away. Virtual love is like that mysterious box of chocolates you get on Valentine's Day—sometimes you bite into a delightful caramel, and other times, you're left chewing on something that resembles a rubber band. Online dating apps have turned the pursuit of romance into a digital scavenger hunt where the only thing you can find with certainty is a plethora of blurry selfies and a few unsolicited cat pictures. Ah, modern love!

Navigating the world of virtual relationships is akin to walking through a minefield while blindfolded and wearing roller skates. You swipe right, and suddenly you're in a whirlwind of emojis, memes, and awkward small talk about the weather. Why is it that every single person seems to love hiking, even if they've never stepped outside their apartment? It's as though the great outdoors has become a virtual myth, like Bigfoot or that one friend who actually enjoys doing their taxes. But here's the kicker: all that digital chatting can lead to some surprisingly deep connections—assuming you don't accidentally send a heart emoji to your boss.

Then comes the moment you decide to take the plunge and meet in person. The thrill of anticipation is only matched by the sheer terror of realizing you might have misrepresented yourself just a tad. Did you really mention that you once ran a marathon when you actually just ran to the fridge during a Netflix binge? The pressure is on, and suddenly your online persona must transform into a real-life human being. Spoiler alert: it's not always a seamless transition. You may find that your date shows up looking like a supermodel while you resemble a raccoon that just emerged from an all-night pizza party.

Of course, virtual love is not without its benefits. You can date while wearing sweatpants, and nobody is the wiser. There's something incredibly liberating about being able to enjoy a romantic dinner over a video call, with the only thing on your mind being whether you can successfully hide your messy living room from the camera. And let's not forget about those heartwarming late-night conversations that can range from philosophical debates about the meaning of life to arguments over the best pizza toppings. Who knew love could come with such a side of pineapple?

As we navigate this quirky landscape of virtual love, it's essential to remember that despite the digital barriers, the core of human connection remains the same. Whether your heart is ensconced in a pixelated format or bursting forth in real-life encounters, love is still love—complete with its own sweet and sour moments. So, embrace the adventure, laugh at the mishaps, and keep your heart open. After all, you never know when the next click might lead you to a love story worth telling—complete with all the awkward pauses and delightful surprises that come with it.

Lessons Learned the Hard Way

The Ex Files: What Not to Do Again

In the wild world of romance, the Ex Files serve as a warning beacon for those brave enough to navigate the treacherous waters of love. Picture this: you're cruising along on the love boat, and suddenly, there's an iceberg labeled "Ex." It's not just any iceberg; it's the one that sunk the Titanic. So, let's dive into the hilariously cringe-worthy lessons learned from past relationships that should come with a "do not repeat" sign.

First up, we have the classic blunder of the "Texting Ex." You know, the one where you're feeling all warm and fuzzy after a few too many glasses of wine and decide it's a brilliant idea to send a heartfelt message to your former flame. Spoiler alert: It's never a good idea. If your ex is on your mind post-wine, it's probably a sign that you should be hitting the gym instead of the "send" button. Trust me, the only thing you'll achieve is a new level of embarrassment and a new reason to block them on social media.

Next on our list is the "Over-Analysis Olympics." This is where you dissect every word, emoji, and punctuation mark from your last conversation like it's a Shakespearean sonnet. You might think

84

you're Sherlock Holmes on the case of "What Did They Mean?" but in reality, you're more like a raccoon rummaging through trash. Instead of gaining clarity, you gain a headache and a new appreciation for ice cream. Remember, if you find yourself crafting a flowchart to decipher your ex's behavior, it's time to put the magnifying glass down and step away from the drama.

Let's not forget about the "Social Media Stalker" phase. You know, the one where you've turned into a detective, scrolling through every photo and post your ex has made since your breakup like it's the latest season of your favorite show. You're not just a casual observer; you're an undercover agent with a mission. The results? A cocktail of jealousy, confusion, and the realization that maybe you should have just invested that time in learning a new hobby. Spoiler: your ex is not going to change their mind because you liked their 5-month-old vacation photo.

Now, we arrive at the "Rebound Regret." This is the moment you think dating someone new will magically erase your ex from your mind. But here's the catch: if you're still hung up on your previous relationship, your new partner is likely to feel like a placeholder, and that's not fair to anyone involved. You're not a vending machine where you can just swap out one snack for another. Take the time to heal, and don't drag someone else into your emotional baggage claim. Trust me, nobody wants to be the emotional equivalent of a third wheel.

In the end, every misstep in the Ex Files is an opportunity to learn and laugh at our past selves. Love is a journey full of bumps, bruises, and plenty of awkward moments. The key is to take those experiences, wrap them up in a humorous bow, and move forward with the wisdom that comes from knowing exactly what not to do again. So, let's raise a glass to our past loves—may they forever remain in the archives of "What Not to Do Again."

The "We Need to Talk" Moment: A Comedy of Timing

There's a universal truth in relationships: the "We Need to Talk" moment is like a surprise party you never wanted but can't escape. You know that feeling when your partner suddenly shifts from casual banter to a serious tone, and your stomach drops faster than a roller coaster? It's as if they've just revealed that the last slice of pizza has been thrown away. The timing is always impeccable—right after you've binge-watched a series on love and romance, only to find yourself knee-deep in a conversation that feels more like a trip to the dentist than a heart-to-heart.

Picture this: you're snuggled up on the couch, popcorn in hand, and your partner looks at you with those big, innocent eyes. You think they're about to confess their undying love, but instead, you get, "We need to talk." Suddenly, the romantic music in your head turns into a suspenseful thriller score. You go from dreaming of sunsets on a beach to imagining a courtroom drama where you're the defendant. Who knew love could feel like a legal proceeding? The stakes are high, and your mind races through a checklist of possible crimes against love you might have committed, including eating their leftover fries or forgetting their birthday.

Timing, of course, is everything. The classic "We Need to Talk" moment usually strikes when you least expect it—like when you're still half-asleep and trying to figure out if the person in front of you is your partner or a very confused burglar. Why do these conversations never happen after a romantic dinner? They seem to lurk in the shadows, waiting for the precise moment when you've just let your guard down. It's as if the universe has a twisted sense of humor, orchestrating these scenarios for maximum comedic effect. You can almost hear the laugh track playing in the background as you scramble to keep the conversation from spiraling into chaos.

Then comes the dreaded question: "What's wrong?" You try to recall if you left the toilet seat up or if you've been hogging the remote control. But the reality is, the "What's wrong?" moment often leads to a rabbit hole of misunderstandings. One minute you're talking about your Netflix queue, and the next, you're debating whether leaving the dishes in the sink constitutes a declaration of war. It's as if love has a hidden manual that no one gives you, filled with rules that change daily and are often open to interpretation. The beauty of it all, however, is that these moments, while fraught with tension, often lead to the funniest stories later on, once everyone has calmed down and had a good laugh.

In the end, the "We Need to Talk" moment serves as a reminder that love isn't just about the rosy sunsets and candlelit dinners. It's about navigating the awkward, the absurd, and the downright hilarious aspects of sharing your life with another human being. So the next time you find yourself in one of those cringe-worthy conversations, take a deep breath and try to find the humor in it. After all, love is what it is—a wild ride filled with unexpected twists, and sometimes, you just have to laugh your way through the confusion.

Moving On: How to Laugh at Your Past

Moving on from our past can feel like trying to fit into last year's jeans: it's uncomfortable, awkward, and sometimes downright impossible. We've all been there, right? You're scrolling through old photos, and suddenly you're confronted with a picture of yourself in a questionable hairstyle or a fashion choice that should have been left in the depths of the closet. The key to moving on is learning to laugh at these moments. Yes, those embarrassing memories can become the punchlines of your life's stand-up routine. Instead of cringing, embrace the absurdity of your past choices; after all, they make for great stories at parties!

Let's be real: we've all had that phase where we thought we were the next great romantic hero, only to discover we were actually more of a romantic zero. Remember that time you tried to win over your crush with a grand gesture, like serenading them in public? Spoiler alert: it usually doesn't end well. The ability to look back on these moments with humor is liberating. It's like a mental detox for your heart. You're not just shedding the weight of past relationships; you're also shedding the embarrassment of those cringe-worthy attempts at love. So, go ahead and chuckle at your younger self. They were trying their best, but they probably also believed that wearing socks with sandals was a bold fashion statement.

As you sift through the memories, you'll notice a pattern: the recurring bad dates, the awkward conversations, and the moments that make you question your judgment. Instead of wallowing in self-pity, turn those experiences into comedy gold. Share them with friends over drinks. Nothing bonds people quite like laughter over shared relationships failures. Plus, you might find that others are eager to share their own hilariously disastrous tales. This collective chuckling not only helps you heal but also reminds you that you're not alone. Everyone has a past filled with questionable decisions and a few regrettable haircuts.

The art of moving on is also about recognizing that your past doesn't define you. Sure, you might have made some cringeworthy choices, but those moments are merely chapters in your love story. They add richness and flavor, like the weird ingredient in your favorite dish that you can't quite place but makes it extraordinary. So, every time you feel tempted to dwell on what went wrong, remind yourself that these experiences are what make you relatable. They're the seasoning that adds depth to your character. Plus, let's face it, who doesn't love a good underdog story?

Ultimately, learning to laugh at your past is a powerful tool in your journey toward love. It allows you to approach new relationships with a light heart and an open mind. When you're not weighed down by the baggage of yesterday, you create space for the possibilities of tomorrow. So, the next time you find yourself reminiscing about that awkward first date or the time you accidentally texted your ex instead of your best friend, chuckle, take a deep breath, and remember: love is a wild ride, and sometimes, the best way to enjoy the journey is to laugh at the bumps along the way.

The Joy of Lasting Love

The Comfort of Routine: When Boring is Beautiful

In a world that constantly bombards us with excitement and novelty, it's easy to overlook the charm of routine. Picture this: you wake up, brew your coffee, and settle into your favorite chair. The sun filters through the window, and the smell of toast wafts through the air. It might sound like a scene from a sitcom, but these seemingly mundane moments are where the magic happens. Routine is like that dependable friend who always shows up with snacks at the party—unassuming yet essential. Who needs roller coasters when you can ride the wave of a perfectly timed 7:00 AM coffee?

Now, let's address the elephant in the room: the word "boring." It's a term that often gets a bad rap, as if it's the villain in a romantic comedy. But consider this: boring is the unsung hero of love. It's the predictable rhythm that allows us to dance together without stepping on each other's toes. In relationships, the beauty of routine is akin to that favorite song you could play on repeat without getting tired of it. Those Saturday mornings spent in pajamas, arguing over the best way to make scrambled eggs, might not make headlines, but they certainly build a solid foundation for love to flourish.

Embracing routine means saying yes to the little things that add up to a whole lot of love. Think of it as the equivalent of wearing your most comfortable sweatpants on a Friday night instead of squeezing into those unforgiving jeans. There's nothing glamorous about eating takeout while binge-watching your favorite show, yet it's in those moments that you often find the deepest connections. Who knew that arguing over which movie to watch or fighting for the last piece of pizza could be the glue that holds your relationship together? It's practically a comedy sketch waiting to happen!

Of course, there will always be moments when spontaneity seems more appealing. Who doesn't want to be swept off their feet by a surprise trip to Paris? But let's face it: the chances of getting caught in traffic or battling a language barrier often overshadow the romance of the unexpected. Routine offers a comforting predictability that allows love to thrive without the anxiety of planning the next big adventure. After all, nothing says "I love you" quite like knowing what your partner's favorite pizza topping is and being ready with an extra slice.

In the grand scheme of love, the beauty of routine lies in its ability to create a safe space for vulnerability and growth. It's the blanket fort of relationships, where you can laugh, cry, and share your dreams without fear of judgment. So, the next time you find yourself in a "boring" moment, take a step back and appreciate the beauty in its simplicity. Love may not always be a whirlwind of excitement, but it certainly can be a cozy, delightful routine that warms your heart—preferably while you're both still in your pajamas.

Growing Together: Love After the Honeymoon Phase

Ah, the honeymoon phase—those blissful days when love feels like a never-ending rom-com, complete with cheesy one-liners and spontaneous dance parties in the living room. You know, the time when you could stare into each other's eyes over dinner and talk about your favorite ice cream flavors for hours without a hint of boredom. But as the dust settles and reality sets in, that sparkly sheen can dull a bit, like the aftermath of a wild party where someone forgot to take out the trash. So, how do we transition from the fairytale to the everyday without losing our minds or each other?

First things first: embrace the quirks. You know what I'm talking about—those little idiosyncrasies that seemed endearing when you were head over heels but now seem slightly maddening. Perhaps your partner has a unique method of folding laundry that resembles origami gone wrong, or maybe they insist on putting ketchup on everything. Instead of rolling your eyes and plotting their demise, find the humor in it. Celebrate that oddball personality; let's face it, if life were a sitcom, these moments would be the punchlines. Laughter becomes the glue that helps you navigate the mundane while keeping the love alive.

Next, it's time to redefine your romantic pursuits. Gone are the days of surprise candlelit dinners and spontaneous weekend getaways (at least, for now). But that doesn't mean romance is dead; it just means it's taken on a new form. Picture this: a Friday night Netflix binge with homemade popcorn, or a cooking disaster where you both end up covered in flour but giggling like kids. These simple moments can be just as fulfilling as those grand gestures, and let's be real, who doesn't love a little chaos in the kitchen? It's a bonding experience like no other—plus, you always have the option of ordering pizza when things go awry.

Communication remains your best friend, and no, we're not talking about the "let's sit down and have a serious conversation" kind. Instead, think of it as creating your own secret language. Develop inside jokes that only the two of you understand. This can be anything from silly nicknames to ridiculous hand signals that save you from a full-blown argument in public. The goal is to keep the lines of communication open while adding a dose of playfulness. Who knew that discussing the grocery list could turn into a hilarious debate over whether avocados should be classified as a fruit or a vegetable?

Finally, remember that growing together means accepting change. As time goes on, you might find yourselves evolving in unexpected ways. Maybe you've developed a newfound passion for pottery, and your partner prefers to binge-watch documentaries on the history of cheese (yes, that's a thing). Instead of viewing these differences as a rift, consider them as opportunities for growth. Encourage each other to explore these interests, and who knows, you might just end up with a unique pottery piece that doubles as a cheese platter. It's all about finding that sweet balance between individuality and togetherness, which can be as delicious as a perfectly paired wine and cheese.

In the end, love after the honeymoon phase doesn't have to be a scary descent into the abyss of boredom. By embracing quirks, redefining romance, fostering playful communication, and accepting change, you can create a relationship that's not only fun but also deeply fulfilling. So, grab your partner, share a laugh, and remember: love is what it is, and it's often a lot more entertaining than any movie could portray.

Celebrating Love: The Little Things that Matter Most

In the grand scheme of love, it's the little things that often steal the spotlight and make our hearts do a little jig. You know, those moments that don't require a grand gesture or a five-star restaurant reservation. Like when your partner brings you a cup of coffee just the way you like it—hot, strong, and with just enough cream to make the barista jealous. You might find yourself thinking, "Is this love, or is it just really good coffee?" Spoiler alert: it's both! It's those caffeine-fueled acts of kindness that remind us love can be as simple as a well-timed caffeine fix.

Let's not forget the magic found in shared inside jokes. You know you've hit the love jackpot when you and your partner can communicate in a series of quirky looks and nonsensical phrases that make absolutely no sense to anyone else. Whether it's a silly nickname or a hilarious mishap from last summer's camping trip, these little snippets of shared humor create a bond that feels unbreakable. It's like having a secret language that only you two speak, which is equal parts adorable and slightly absurd. And honestly, who wouldn't want to explain to their friends why they can't stop laughing over "the great spaghetti incident of 2020"?

Then there are the spontaneous dance parties in the living room, which are the unsung heroes of love celebrations. Picture this: you're folding laundry, and suddenly your favorite song comes on. Instead of just nodding your head in rhythm while sorting socks, your partner grabs your hand, and within seconds, you're spinning around the room like you're auditioning for a musical. Sure, you might trip over the dog or knock a lamp over, but what's love without a little chaos? Those moments remind us that love doesn't have to be serious; it can be silly, spontaneous, and full of laughter.

Speaking of laughter, there's nothing quite like the joy of sharing food. Whether it's splitting a ridiculously oversized slice of pizza or engaging in a heated debate over the last piece of chocolate cake, food has a magical way of bringing people together. It's in those moments of culinary chaos where love thrives. You might find yourselves fighting over the breadsticks or making a mess trying to cook a new recipe. But at the end of the day, it's not about the food but the memories created—like the time you almost set the kitchen on fire trying to impress your partner with your "culinary skills."

Finally, let's talk about those mundane moments that somehow become extraordinary. When you sit together on the couch, watching your favorite show for the fifth time, or when you're both too lazy to move and decide that pizza delivery is the best plan of action. These seemingly insignificant instances are where love truly flourishes. They remind us that love is not just about grand declarations or candlelit dinners but also about finding comfort in the ordinary. So, celebrate those little things, because in the end, it's the quirks, the laughter, and those perfectly imperfect moments that make love what it is—wonderful, messy, and oh-so-precious.

IGNITE YOUR POTENTIAL

BREAK FREE FROM THE ORDINARY

GEORGE HATCHER

Introduction

Let's be clear from the very beginning: this is not a book written by a motivational expert. You will not find bullet-pointed lists of life hacks, nor will you hear from a guru standing on a mountaintop, dispensing universal truths. I am not an authority on how you should live your life. Far from it. For a significant portion of my own journey, I was an authority on how *not* to live, a case study in the destructive power of ambition when it's untethered from wisdom and foresight. What I do know, what I have earned through decades of trial and error—and some spectacular, life-altering failures—is the nature of my own self-motivation. It has been the engine of my life, a constant fire that has, at different times, either burned my world to the ground or illuminated a path toward a stable, meaningful existence.

This book is a tale of two lives, both lived by the same man. The first half was a storm. It was driven by a relentless, almost primal urge to achieve, to have, to conquer. When I was a young man, if I wanted something, my mindset was simple: "I'm going to have this, no matter what." That single-mindedness propelled me forward, allowing me to build businesses from scratch and expand them with breathtaking speed. But the "no matter what" came with a hidden clause, a price I didn't fully comprehend until the bill came due. I paid for that recklessness dearly. Without capital, I fueled my expansion with bad checks, building a sprawling enterprise on a foundation of fraud. Was it because my brain was fried from the sheer amount of alcohol I was consuming in those days? I can't say for sure, but the decisions I made were not those of a sound mind. That path didn't lead to lasting glory; it led, as it inevitably must, to a jail cell.

The stories in my earlier books, the *Pages of Passion* series, detail that chaotic first life. It was a life of chasing, of running, of flying too close to the sun and crashing back to earth. What you are holding now is an exploration of what came after the crash. It's about the second half of my life—a period now spanning more than thirty-eight years—where the fire of motivation didn't die out, but was instead channeled. The bumps in the road never disappear entirely, because life itself can be bumpy, but the self-inflicted chaos vanished.

In this second life, I reinvented myself. The same drive that had once pushed me into illegal schemes was redirected. I found a new calling, one that came looking for me: I became a trusted advisor to lawyers, a specialist in the delicate arts of client development and management. I discovered a "magic" in building relationships and managing expectations, guiding legal cases for clients across the country from afar. I still built businesses along the way, but they were different. They were built on solid ground, with thought, integrity, and patience—virtues I had little time for in my youth. I certainly didn't write any bad checks to get them started.

This book, then, is not the complete story of my life. That ongoing, raw, and detailed narrative can be found in my *Pages of Passion* series. Think of *this* book as something different: my own humble motivational guide, born from the wreckage and reconstruction of a life lived at extremes. The principles laid out in these pages—from shifting your mindset to building resilience and aligning your actions with your values—are the very lessons I learned through decades of struggle and reinvention. I don't want you to make the same mistakes I did. My hope is that by sharing my story first, you might gain some perspective on your own journey, on your own fire, and on the critical importance of deciding not just *what* you want to build, but *how* you choose to build it.

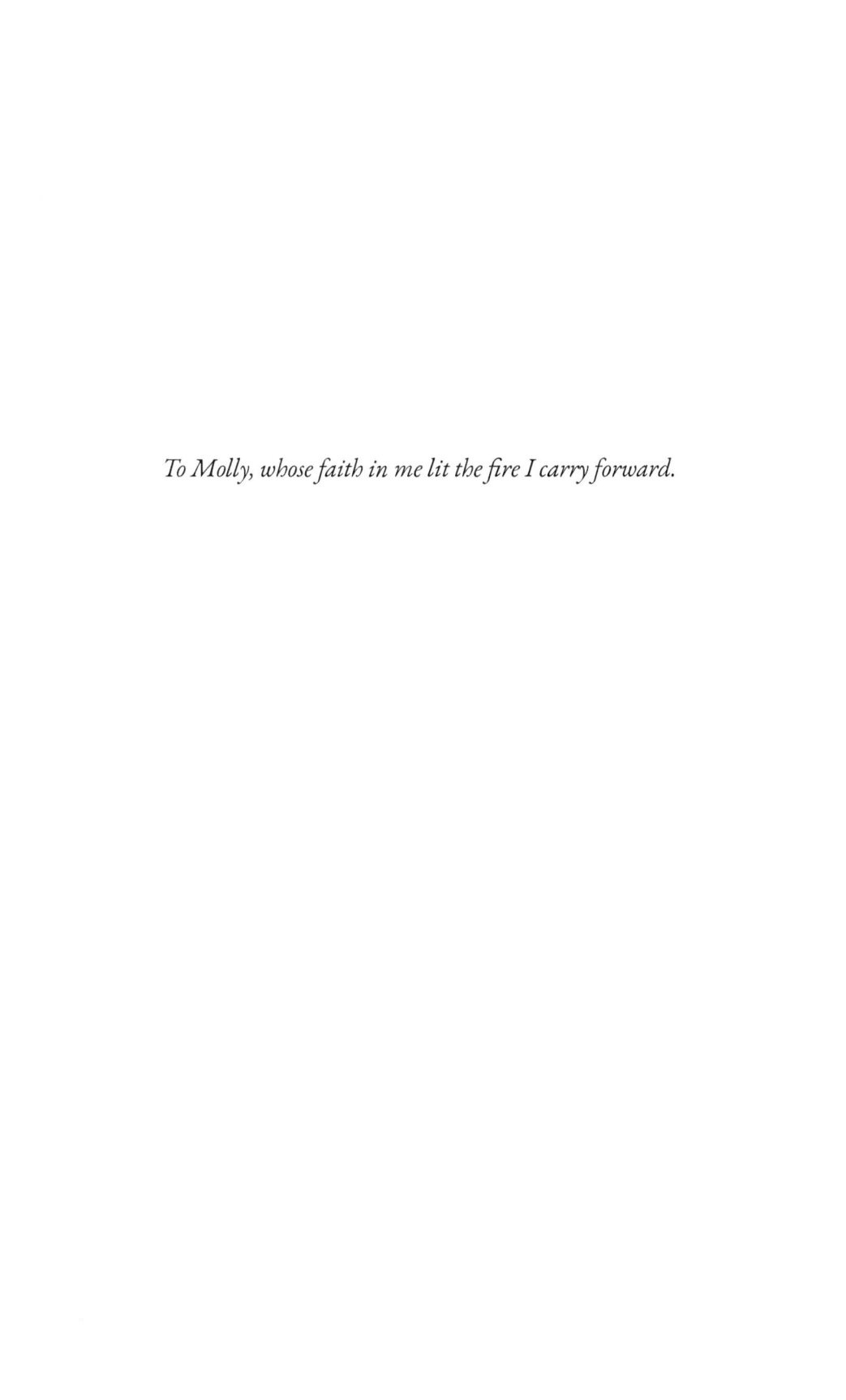

To Molly, whose faith in me lit the fire I carry forward.

Chapter 1: Awakening the Fire Within

～～∽⌒

Discovering Your Why

Finding your purpose is a transformative journey that can breathe new life into your daily routine. Many people feel stuck in their lives, going through the motions without a clear sense of direction. This feeling of stagnation can lead to boredom and dissatisfaction. However, discovering your "why" can ignite a spark that propels you toward a more meaningful existence.

To uncover your "why," start by reflecting on your passions and interests. What activities make you lose track of time? What topics ignite your curiosity? These questions can help you identify what truly resonates with you. By focusing on what you love, you can begin to align your actions with your values and desires, creating a pathway toward a more fulfilling life.

Additionally, consider the impact you want to have on the world around you. Think about the legacy you wish to leave behind. Understanding how you want to contribute can provide clarity and motivation. When your actions are guided by a deeper purpose, even mundane tasks can feel significant, transforming your day-to-day activities into stepping stones toward your greater goals.

It's important to be patient and open during this exploration process. Discovering your "why" is not an overnight achievement; it requires introspection and experimentation. Allow yourself to try new things, meet different people, and explore various interests. Each experience will bring you closer to understanding your true purpose.

Finally, once you have a clearer sense of your "why," embrace it fully. Share it with others and let it guide your decisions. This newfound clarity can serve as a powerful motivator, helping you break free from the ordinary and pursue a life filled with passion and meaning. Remember, your journey is uniquely yours, and every step taken toward your purpose is a testament to your commitment to living an extraordinary life.

Embracing Change

Embracing change is a fundamental step toward unlocking your true potential. When you find yourself bored with the monotony of daily routines, it signifies a deeper yearning for growth and fulfillment. Change can be intimidating, but it is also an opportunity to discover new paths that lead to meaningful experiences. By shifting your mindset and viewing change as a chance for improvement, you can ignite the passion within you and propel yourself toward a more vibrant life.

To embrace change effectively, begin by identifying what aspects of your life feel stagnant. Acknowledging these feelings allows you to take proactive steps toward transformation. Whether it's changing your career, exploring new hobbies, or altering your daily habits, every small change adds up. It is crucial to cultivate a sense of curiosity about the world around you and to remain open to new experiences that can enrich your life.

As you embark on this journey of embracing change, remember that discomfort is often a sign of growth. The initial stages of change may bring uncertainty and fear, but these feelings are natural. Allow yourself to feel these emotions without letting them dictate your actions. Surround yourself with supportive individuals who encourage your growth and share their own experiences of change, as this can provide both inspiration and assurance.

The process of embracing change also requires you to set clear intentions. Determine what you want to achieve and visualize the outcome. This clarity will serve as a roadmap, guiding you as you navigate through challenges. Keep in mind that setbacks are part of the journey; they do not define your progress but rather contribute to your resilience and adaptability.

Ultimately, embracing change is about making a conscious decision to seek a more meaningful existence. By stepping out of your comfort zone and welcoming new possibilities, you ignite a spark that can lead to profound personal development. Remember, the journey is just as important as the destination, so celebrate your progress and remain committed to continuous growth as you break free from the ordinary.

Chapter 2: Shifting Your Mindset

Overcoming Limiting Beliefs

Overcoming limiting beliefs is a crucial step toward unlocking your true potential. These beliefs often stem from past experiences, societal conditioning, or negative self-talk, creating barriers that keep us from pursuing our dreams. To break free from the ordinary, it's essential to recognize these beliefs and challenge them head-on. This process begins with self-reflection, allowing you to identify the thoughts that hold you back, such as "I'm not good enough" or "I'll never succeed."

Once you've identified these beliefs, the next step is to reframe them. Instead of viewing setbacks as failures, consider them opportunities for growth. Adopting a growth mindset can be transformative; it shifts your perspective from one of limitation to one of possibility. As you practice this reframing, you'll start to see that your perceived obstacles can actually become stepping stones toward something greater.

Surrounding yourself with positive influences is another powerful strategy for overcoming limiting beliefs. Engage with individuals who inspire you, whether through books, podcasts, or conversations. Their stories of triumph can serve as motivation, reminding you that change is possible. Additionally, seek out communities that foster personal development; being part of a supportive network can reinforce your commitment to overcoming obstacles.

Visualization techniques can also play a vital role in overcoming limiting beliefs. By vividly imagining your desired outcomes, you create a mental image of success that can motivate you to take action. Picture yourself achieving your goals, experiencing the emotions associated with that success. This practice can help solidify your belief in your capabilities, pushing you to take the necessary steps toward meaningful change.

Finally, remember that overcoming limiting beliefs is a journey, not a destination. Celebrate your progress, no matter how small, and be patient with yourself. Growth takes time, and every step forward is a victory. Stay committed to your personal development, and you will find that the ordinary can become extraordinary, opening doors to a life filled with purpose and fulfillment.

Cultivating a Growth Mindset

Cultivating a growth mindset is essential for anyone looking to break free from the ordinary and embrace a life filled with meaning and purpose. It begins with recognizing that your abilities and intelligence can be developed through dedication and hard work. This perspective fosters resilience, encourages effort, and creates a love for learning, which is vital for personal development. By shifting your mindset, you open yourself up to new possibilities and experiences that can transform your daily routine.

One key aspect of nurturing a growth mindset is embracing challenges instead of avoiding them. When you face obstacles head-on, you learn valuable lessons that pave the way for future success. Each challenge you encounter is an opportunity for growth, as it pushes you out of your comfort zone and helps you discover your true potential. Instead of fearing failure, view it as a stepping stone toward achieving your goals and aspirations.

Another important factor is surrounding yourself with a supportive community. Engaging with like-minded individuals who share your desire for personal growth can significantly impact your journey. These connections provide encouragement, motivation, and constructive feedback that can help you stay focused on your path. Together, you can celebrate victories and learn from setbacks, reinforcing the belief that growth is a continuous process.

Moreover, practicing self-reflection and mindfulness can help you cultivate a growth mindset. Take time to assess your thoughts and feelings, and challenge any limiting beliefs that may hold you back. By being aware of your internal dialogue, you can replace negative thoughts with empowering affirmations that inspire action. This practice not only enhances your self-awareness but also strengthens your resolve to pursue meaningful change in your life.

Finally, remember that cultivating a growth mindset is a lifelong journey. It requires patience, persistence, and a commitment to personal development. As you embrace this mindset, you'll find that each small step taken leads to greater fulfillment and a deeper sense of purpose. By igniting your potential and fostering a growth mindset, you can truly break free from the ordinary and create a life that resonates with your deepest desires and aspirations.

Chapter 3: Setting Meaningful Goals

~~~

Defining Success on Your Terms

Success is a personal journey, unique to each individual. It is essential to define what success means to you, rather than allowing societal expectations or the opinions of others to dictate your path. Take a moment to reflect on what truly matters in your life. Consider your passions, values, and the legacy you wish to leave behind. When you embrace your definition of success, you empower yourself to pursue it wholeheartedly.

Many people feel stuck in their daily routines, yearning for something more meaningful. This stagnation often stems from a lack of clarity regarding personal goals. To ignite your potential, start by setting specific, achievable objectives that align with your vision of success. Break these goals down into manageable steps, and celebrate your progress along the way. Remember, each small victory brings you closer to your ultimate destination.

As you embark on this journey, it's important to cultivate a positive mindset. Surround yourself with supportive individuals who inspire you and share your aspirations. Engage in practices that boost your confidence, such as affirmations or visualizations.

By maintaining a focus on your goals and the reasons behind them, you will find the motivation to push through challenges and setbacks.

Moreover, be open to change and adaptable in your approach. The path to success is rarely linear, and obstacles may arise unexpectedly. Embrace these challenges as opportunities for growth and learning. Each experience, whether positive or negative, contributes to your understanding of yourself and your unique definition of success.

Ultimately, defining success on your terms is about living authentically and pursuing what brings you joy and fulfillment. It's about crafting a life that reflects your true self and aspirations. As you navigate your journey, stay committed to your vision, and remember that success is not just a destination but a continuous process of growth and self-discovery.

Creating an Actionable Plan

Creating an actionable plan is the cornerstone of transforming your aspirations into reality. It begins with identifying specific goals that resonate with your desire for personal growth and meaning. Instead of vague ambitions, break down your goals into clear, achievable tasks. This clarity not only fuels motivation but also provides a roadmap to follow, making the journey less daunting and more focused.

Next, prioritize your tasks based on urgency and importance. This step ensures that you dedicate your energy to what truly matters, preventing the overwhelm that often accompanies change. By tackling one task at a time, you build momentum and confidence, paving the way for further action. Remember, every small step taken is a victory that brings you closer to your larger vision.

As you move forward, it's crucial to set deadlines for your tasks. Deadlines create a sense of urgency and accountability, which can significantly enhance your productivity. They help you maintain focus and track your progress, allowing you to adjust your plan as necessary. Flexibility is key; if something isn't working, don't be afraid to reassess and alter your approach.

Additionally, seek support from those around you. Sharing your goals with friends, family, or mentors can provide encouragement and valuable insights. They can hold you accountable and offer different perspectives that may enhance your plan. Remember, you are not alone in this journey; collaboration can often lead to greater achievements than going solo.

Finally, celebrate your achievements, no matter how small. Recognizing your progress is vital for maintaining motivation and reinforcing your commitment to your goals. By acknowledging each step forward, you cultivate a positive mindset that fuels further action. Your journey toward a more meaningful life is not just about the destination, but also the growth you experience along the way.

Chapter 4: Building Resilience

〜〜

The Power of Perseverance

Perseverance is the cornerstone of success and personal growth. It is the unwavering determination to keep pushing forward, even when the path is riddled with obstacles. For those feeling stuck in monotony, embracing perseverance can ignite a spark of motivation that transforms their daily routines into meaningful pursuits. By cultivating this mindset, individuals can break free from the ordinary and embark on journeys that resonate with their true aspirations.

When faced with challenges, it is easy to feel discouraged and contemplate giving up. However, true progress lies in the ability to rise after every fall. Each setback serves as a lesson, an opportunity to reassess goals and strategies. By viewing challenges as stepping stones rather than barriers, individuals can develop resilience. This shift in perspective fosters a sense of purpose and encourages the pursuit of passions that may have been previously overshadowed by routine.

The stories of those who have achieved remarkable feats often highlight their perseverance in the face of adversity. Icons in various fields have demonstrated that the road to success is rarely linear. They faced failures, criticism, and moments of doubt yet continued to strive toward their goals. These narratives serve as powerful reminders that perseverance is not just about enduring; it is about growing stronger with each challenge encountered along the way.

Engaging in personal development through perseverance also means setting realistic and meaningful goals. It requires patience and the understanding that significant change doesn't happen overnight. By breaking down larger aspirations into manageable steps, individuals can maintain motivation as they witness their progress. Celebrating small victories along the way reinforces the belief that they are capable of achieving great things, further fueling their desire to persevere.

Ultimately, the power of perseverance lies in its ability to transform ordinary lives into extraordinary journeys. It empowers individuals to step out of their comfort zones and pursue endeavors that resonate with their purpose. As they cultivate this vital trait, they unlock their potential and inspire those around them to do the same. The journey may be challenging, but the rewards of perseverance are immeasurable, leading to a life filled with meaning and fulfillment.

Learning from Failure

Failure is often viewed as a setback, but it can actually be one of the most powerful teachers in our lives. When we encounter failure, we are confronted with our limitations and the need to reassess our strategies. This process of reflection is crucial for personal growth. Rather than allowing failure to define us, we can choose to see it as an opportunity to learn and evolve. Embracing this mindset can transform our approach to challenges and inspire us to pursue our goals more passionately.

Each failure carries valuable lessons that can steer us in new directions. It forces us to analyze what went wrong and why, providing insights that success often does not. For instance, when we fail at a particular task, we gain a deeper understanding of our skills and the areas where we need improvement. This awareness is essential for anyone seeking to break free from monotony and find more meaningful pursuits in life. By dissecting our failures, we can identify patterns and develop strategies that align more closely with our true aspirations.

Moreover, many successful individuals attribute their achievements to their experiences with failure. Icons like J.K. Rowling and Thomas Edison faced numerous rejections and setbacks before reaching their goals. Their stories illustrate that resilience in the face of failure is a key ingredient for success. When we recognize that failure is a shared experience among high achievers, it can motivate us to persist through our own obstacles. This realization helps foster a culture of perseverance and a belief in our potential to achieve greatness.

The road to personal development is fraught with challenges, and learning from failure is a crucial part of that journey. It encourages us to step outside of our comfort zones and take risks. Every attempt, whether successful or not, adds to our experience and builds our confidence. By adopting a growth mindset, we can redefine our relationship with failure, viewing it as a stepping stone rather than a stumbling block.

In conclusion, learning from failure is not just about acknowledging mistakes; it is about using those experiences to fuel our personal development. As we advance in our lives, the lessons learned from our failures can guide us toward more fulfilling and meaningful pursuits. By embracing the insights gained from our setbacks, we empower ourselves to create a life that resonates with our true desires and aspirations. So, let us welcome failure as a mentor and move forward with renewed vigor and purpose.

Chapter 5: Breaking Free From Routine

~~~

Identifying Your Comfort Zones

Identifying your comfort zones is the first step toward breaking free from the ordinary. Many individuals find themselves stuck in routines that may feel safe but offer little fulfillment. These comfort zones can be physical, emotional, or mental spaces where familiarity breeds complacency. Acknowledging these zones is crucial for anyone looking to advance and create a more meaningful life.

To begin this process, take a moment to reflect on your daily habits and routines. What activities do you engage in that feel comfortable but unchallenging? Perhaps you have a favorite coffee shop you visit every morning or a predictable work schedule that never varies. By pinpointing these comforting patterns, you can start to understand how they may be holding you back from exploring new opportunities.

Next, consider the emotions tied to your comfort zones. Are there particular feelings you associate with stepping outside your norm? Fear of failure, anxiety about the unknown, or even the simple dread of change can keep you anchored to familiar territory.

Recognizing these emotional barriers is essential, as it allows you to confront them head-on and understand their impact on your desire for growth.

Once you've identified these zones, challenge yourself to step outside of them, even if just slightly. This could mean trying a new hobby, meeting new people, or taking on a different project at work. Each small push against your comfort zone can build confidence and show you that discomfort can lead to growth and opportunity. Embrace the idea that stepping outside your comfort zone is not just a challenge, but a pathway to discovering what truly fulfills you.

Ultimately, identifying your comfort zones is about empowerment. It's about recognizing that while comfort can feel safe, it can also become a barrier to your potential. By acknowledging and challenging these zones, you open the door to a more dynamic and meaningful existence. Remember, every step you take toward discomfort is a step toward igniting your potential and reshaping your life.

Exploring New Opportunities

In a world that often feels monotonous, the quest for new opportunities can ignite the spark of inspiration within us. Many individuals find themselves trapped in a cycle of routine, longing for something more fulfilling. This chapter invites you to explore the vast landscape of possibilities that lie beyond your current situation. Embracing change and seeking new experiences can lead to personal growth and a renewed sense of purpose.

The first step in exploring new opportunities is recognizing the potential for change that exists in every moment. Whether it's a new hobby, a career shift, or simply altering your daily habits, each choice you make can open doors to exciting prospects. By stepping outside your comfort zone, you can discover hidden talents and passions that have been waiting to be unearthed. The journey of self-discovery begins when you dare to take that first leap into the unknown.

Networking and connecting with others can also play a crucial role in uncovering new opportunities. Engaging with people who share similar interests or who have ventured into different fields can provide valuable insights and inspiration. These connections can lead to collaborations that spark creativity and innovation, paving the way for unique paths you may not have considered before. Remember, every conversation is a chance to learn something new and expand your horizons.

Additionally, setting clear goals can guide your exploration of opportunities. By defining what you want to achieve, you create a roadmap that helps you measure progress and stay motivated. Goals serve as a constant reminder of your aspirations, ensuring that you remain focused on your journey toward a more meaningful existence. Celebrate small victories along the way, as they are stepping stones toward larger achievements.

Finally, maintaining a positive mindset is essential when exploring new opportunities. Challenges will arise, but viewing them as learning experiences rather than setbacks can transform your perspective. Embrace the idea that every experience, whether successful or not, contributes to your growth. As you navigate through your journey, remember that the pursuit of new opportunities is not just about changing your circumstances but about evolving into the best version of yourself.

Chapter 6: Harnessing Your Passion

Finding What Sets Your Soul on Fire

Finding what sets your soul on fire is an essential journey toward personal fulfillment. It's about identifying those passions and interests that resonate deeply within you, igniting a sense of purpose and enthusiasm. Many people find themselves stuck in a monotonous routine, feeling unfulfilled and yearning for something more significant. This chapter encourages you to explore the depths of your desires and dreams, paving the way for a more meaningful existence.

To begin this exploration, take a moment to reflect on what truly excites you. What activities make you lose track of time? What topics can you talk about for hours without feeling drained? By identifying these sparks of joy, you can start to piece together the puzzle of your passions. Remember, this journey is not merely about finding a career or hobby; it's about connecting with your authentic self and understanding what brings you genuine happiness.

Consider the moments in your life when you felt the most alive. Was it during a creative endeavor, a moment of connection with others, or perhaps an adventure in nature? These memories can serve as guiding lights, helping you navigate toward what truly sets your soul on fire. Embrace these experiences and learn from them; they are clues pointing you toward a more fulfilling path.

Additionally, don't shy away from trying new things. Sometimes, stepping outside your comfort zone can lead to unexpected discoveries. Attend workshops, join clubs, or volunteer for causes that resonate with you. Each new experience is a chance to uncover hidden interests and passions. The more you explore, the clearer your vision of what ignites your spirit will become.

Finally, be patient with yourself. Finding what sets your soul on fire is a journey, not a destination. It requires introspection, experimentation, and sometimes even trial and error. Allow yourself the grace to evolve and grow through this process. As you embark on this transformative journey, remember that the pursuit of passion is a deeply personal endeavor, and every step you take brings you closer to a more vibrant and meaningful life.

Turning Passion into Purpose

Many individuals find themselves trapped in a cycle of monotony, yearning for something more than the daily grind. This is where the journey of turning passion into purpose begins. Recognizing what ignites your enthusiasm is the first step toward transforming your life. It's essential to reflect on what activities make you lose track of time and fill you with joy, as these passions can guide you toward a more fulfilling existence.

Once you have identified your passions, the next step is to align them with your core values and beliefs. Passion alone is not enough; it must be rooted in a purpose that resonates with who you are at your core. Take the time to explore what truly matters to you and how your unique interests can serve a greater good. When you find the intersection of passion and purpose, you unlock the potential for a deeply meaningful life.

Setting goals is crucial in this transformative process. Goals provide a roadmap to turn your passion into actionable steps. Start small by setting achievable milestones that lead you closer to your ultimate vision. Celebrate each victory, no matter how minor, as these moments of progress fuel your motivation and reinforce your commitment to your purpose.

Embracing a growth mindset will help you navigate the challenges you may encounter along the way. Understand that setbacks are a natural part of any journey. Each obstacle presents an opportunity to learn and grow. By viewing challenges as stepping stones rather than barriers, you can maintain your momentum and continue moving toward your goals with determination and resilience.

Finally, surround yourself with a supportive community that shares your vision. Engaging with like-minded individuals can provide encouragement, inspiration, and accountability. Seek out mentors and peers who can offer guidance and share their own experiences. Together, you can foster an environment that nurtures your passion and purpose, making the journey not only fulfilling but also enriching.

Chapter 7: Surrounding Yourself with Positivity

The Impact of Your Environment

Your environment plays a crucial role in shaping your mindset and determining your potential. It encompasses everything from the people you surround yourself with to the physical spaces you inhabit. If you find yourself in a setting that stifles creativity or breeds negativity, it can be challenging to break free from the mundane. Conversely, a supportive and inspiring environment can ignite your passions and propel you toward meaningful change. Recognizing the importance of your surroundings is the first step toward transforming your life.

Imagine waking up every day in a space that energizes you, filled with colors, sounds, and people that uplift your spirit. This is not merely about aesthetics; it's about creating an atmosphere that fosters growth and innovation. Seek out environments that challenge you, whether that means joining a new community, attending workshops, or simply rearranging your workspace. By intentionally curating your surroundings, you open the door to new opportunities and perspectives that can dismantle the ordinary.

The people you interact with daily have a profound impact on your motivation and ambitions. Are you surrounded by those who inspire you, or do you find yourself in a circle that reinforces your fears and doubts? Surrounding yourself with positive influences can provide the encouragement you need to step outside your comfort zone. Engage with individuals who share your desire for growth, as their energy and aspirations can be contagious, leading to collaborative efforts that enhance your journey.

Additionally, consider the impact of your physical environment on your mental state. A cluttered, disorganized space can lead to feelings of overwhelm, while a clean, organized area can enhance focus and creativity. Make small changes, like decluttering your desk or adding plants to your workspace, to create a more inviting and stimulating atmosphere. These adjustments can help you cultivate a mindset that is more receptive to new ideas and opportunities.

Finally, remember that your environment is not fixed; it's malleable and can be reshaped according to your aspirations. Take proactive steps to alter your surroundings, whether through changes in your social circles or by seeking out new experiences that align with your goals. By consciously influencing your environment, you empower yourself to break free from the ordinary and embark on a journey of personal development that is rich with meaning and purpose.

Building a Supportive Network

Building a supportive network is crucial for anyone looking to break free from the ordinary and ignite their potential. Surrounding yourself with positive, driven individuals can create an environment that fosters growth and motivation. Each connection you make can open new doors, provide fresh perspectives, and inspire you to take bold steps toward your goals. Embrace the idea that your network can serve as a powerful catalyst for transformation in your life.

To start building this network, focus on finding individuals who share your aspirations and values. Attend workshops, seminars, or community events that align with your interests. Engage in conversations and actively seek out relationships with those who challenge and uplift you. Remember, the quality of your connections is more important than the quantity; a few supportive relationships can be more impactful than a large number of superficial ones.

Don't hesitate to reach out to mentors or role models who have successfully navigated paths similar to the one you aspire to take. Their experiences can provide invaluable insights and guidance, helping you avoid common pitfalls. A mentor can also serve as a source of accountability, encouraging you to stay committed to your journey of personal development and growth.

In addition to seeking out mentors, consider joining groups or organizations that align with your passions. Being part of a community not only provides support but also fosters a sense of belonging. Engaging with like-minded individuals can inspire creativity and collaboration, allowing you to explore different avenues and broaden your horizons in ways you might not have considered before.

Lastly, remember that building a supportive network is an ongoing process. As you evolve, so should your connections. Keep nurturing your relationships, and don't be afraid to reevaluate and expand your network as you grow. By actively engaging with others and fostering meaningful connections, you'll find that your journey toward a more meaningful life becomes not only achievable but also incredibly fulfilling.

Chapter 8: Taking Action

The Importance of Small Steps

In a world that often glorifies grand gestures and monumental changes, it's essential to remember the power of small steps. Each tiny action we take can lead to significant transformations over time. For those feeling stuck in a monotonous routine, embracing these small changes can breathe new life into their daily existence. Rather than waiting for a big, life-altering moment, focusing on incremental progress can create a sense of achievement and motivation.

Taking small steps allows for manageable adjustments that can lead to meaningful growth. Instead of overwhelming oneself with the idea of a complete overhaul, breaking goals into tiny, achievable tasks makes the journey less daunting. This method not only fosters a sense of accomplishment but also builds confidence over time. Each small victory adds up, creating a momentum that propels individuals toward their larger aspirations.

Moreover, small steps encourage consistency, which is crucial for personal development. When actions are broken down into bite-sized pieces, individuals are more likely to stick with them.

This consistency breeds habits that contribute to long-term success. Whether it's reading a few pages of a book daily or taking a short walk each morning, these habits can lead to significant changes in mindset and lifestyle.

Another advantage of small steps is the opportunity for reflection and adjustment. As one progresses through their journey, it's easier to evaluate what works and what doesn't when changes are incremental. This adaptability allows individuals to pivot as necessary, ensuring that their path remains aligned with their evolving goals and desires. Instead of feeling trapped by rigid plans, one can embrace fluidity and respond to their circumstances.

Ultimately, the importance of small steps lies in their ability to transform the ordinary into something extraordinary. For those yearning for meaning and fulfillment in their lives, these incremental changes can serve as stepping stones toward a richer existence. By focusing on small, consistent actions, individuals can cultivate a sense of purpose and direction, igniting their potential to break free from the mundane and embrace a more meaningful life.

Celebrating Progress

Celebrating progress is an essential part of personal development, as it fuels motivation and reinforces the commitment to pursuing meaningful changes. Every step taken toward your goals, no matter how small, deserves recognition. When we acknowledge our achievements, we create a positive feedback loop that encourages us to keep pushing forward and striving for more. This celebration can take many forms, from simply reflecting on your journey to sharing milestones with friends and family who support your growth.

One effective way to celebrate progress is by setting up a personal reward system. By aligning small rewards with your accomplishments, you create a sense of anticipation and excitement around achieving your goals. For instance, after completing a challenging task or reaching a specific milestone, treat yourself to something enjoyable, whether it's a favorite meal, a day out, or even a self-care activity. This not only makes the journey more enjoyable but also reinforces the notion that progress is worth celebrating.

Additionally, documenting your journey can serve as a powerful reminder of how far you've come. Keeping a journal or creating a visual representation of your goals and achievements allows you to look back at your progress with pride. This practice helps to maintain motivation, especially during times when you may feel stuck or discouraged. By revisiting past successes, you can reignite your passion for growth and remind yourself of the potential that lies within.

Sharing your progress with others can also amplify the joy of your accomplishments. By discussing your journey with friends, family, or a supportive community, you create an environment of encouragement and accountability. This social aspect of celebrating progress not only boosts your morale but also inspires those around you to pursue their own meaningful changes. Remember, your story can motivate others who may be feeling lost or unsure about their paths.

Finally, always take a moment to reflect on your journey and acknowledge the hard work you've put in. Celebrating progress isn't just about the end goal; it's about appreciating the growth and learning that occur along the way. Embrace the lessons learned, the challenges faced, and the strength gained. By doing so, you cultivate a mindset geared toward continuous improvement and fulfillment, allowing you to break free from the ordinary and truly ignite your potential.

Chapter 9: Embracing Lifelong Learning

The Benefits of Continuous Growth

Continuous growth is essential for anyone seeking to advance beyond the ordinary. It offers the opportunity to break free from the monotony of daily routines and explore new avenues of personal development. Engaging in continuous growth allows individuals to challenge themselves, fostering resilience and adaptability. This journey not only enhances self-awareness but also cultivates a sense of purpose that is often missing in repetitive lifestyles.

One of the most significant benefits of continuous growth is the boost it provides to motivation. When individuals set new goals and pursue new skills, they ignite a passion for learning that can transform their outlook on life. This intrinsic motivation propels them forward, encouraging them to take risks and embrace change with enthusiasm. In this way, growth becomes a catalyst for a more vibrant and fulfilling life.

Moreover, continuous growth enhances one's ability to overcome obstacles. As people push their boundaries, they develop a toolkit of strategies and mindsets that enable them to face challenges head-on. This resilience is invaluable, as it not only prepares individuals for future difficulties but also instills a deep confidence in their capabilities. With each step taken outside their comfort zones, they reinforce the belief that they can achieve meaningful change.

In addition to personal benefits, a commitment to continuous growth positively impacts relationships. As individuals evolve, they bring fresh perspectives and ideas to their interactions with others. This openness fosters deeper connections and encourages collaboration, which can lead to new opportunities in both personal and professional realms. The ripple effect of one person's growth can inspire those around them to embark on their own journeys of development.

Ultimately, embracing continuous growth is about creating a more meaningful life. It encourages individuals to seek out experiences that align with their values and aspirations, rather than settling for the status quo. By prioritizing personal development, they not only enrich their own lives but also contribute to the collective growth of their communities. With each step taken toward growth, individuals move closer to realizing their full potential, transforming the ordinary into the extraordinary.

Seeking New Experiences

In a world that often feels monotonous, seeking new experiences can be the key to unlocking your true potential. Many individuals find themselves trapped in a cycle of routine, where days blend into one another without distinction. This mundane existence can lead to feelings of dissatisfaction and a yearning for something more meaningful. By actively pursuing new experiences, you can break free from the ordinary and reignite your passion for life.

Exploring new activities, whether they be hobbies, travel, or learning opportunities, can provide fresh perspectives that enrich your life. Each new experience acts as a stepping stone toward personal growth, challenging you to step outside your comfort zone. The thrill of trying something unfamiliar can spark creativity and motivation, igniting a desire to continue seeking out adventures. Embrace the unknown, for it is often in these moments that we discover our true selves.

Additionally, seeking new experiences fosters resilience and adaptability. Life is full of surprises, and the ability to navigate change is crucial for personal development. When you expose yourself to different situations, you build confidence and learn to embrace uncertainty. This ability to adapt not only enhances your personal growth but also equips you with valuable skills that can be applied in various aspects of life, including career advancement.

Moreover, engaging with new experiences allows you to connect with others who share similar interests. Building a network of like-minded individuals can lead to meaningful relationships and collaborations. These connections often provide support and encouragement, further motivating you to pursue your goals. The shared journey of exploration can be incredibly rewarding, as you learn from others while also contributing your own insights and experiences.

In conclusion, seeking new experiences is essential for anyone looking to break free from the mundane and ignite their potential. The journey of personal development is enriched by the willingness to embrace change and explore the unfamiliar. By stepping out of your comfort zone, you open the door to a world filled with opportunities for growth, connection, and fulfillment. Remember, every new experience is a chance to learn, grow, and ultimately, transform your life.

Chapter 10: Living a Meaningful Life

~~~

Aligning Actions with Values

Aligning your actions with your values is a vital step toward achieving a fulfilling life. When you understand what truly matters to you, you can begin to make decisions that resonate with your core beliefs. This alignment not only fosters a sense of purpose but also ignites a passion that drives you to pursue your goals relentlessly. Whether it's personal growth, career changes, or new adventures, living in accordance with your values transforms mundane routines into meaningful journeys.

To start aligning your actions with your values, take time for self-reflection. Identify what you genuinely value in life—be it family, health, creativity, or contribution to society. Write these values down and assess how your current lifestyle reflects them. Are there areas where your actions contradict these values? Recognizing these discrepancies is the first step in making the necessary adjustments that lead to a more authentic existence.

Next, set specific goals that embody your values. For instance, if one of your core values is helping others, you might consider volunteering or pursuing a career in social work. Setting goals that align with your values provides clarity and direction, ensuring that your efforts are not just productive but also meaningful. This alignment fuels motivation and helps you break free from the ordinary, paving the way for a more vibrant and engaged life.

As you commit to aligning your actions with your values, embrace the journey of transformation, even when it's challenging. Change is often uncomfortable, but it is necessary for growth. Surround yourself with supportive individuals who encourage you to stay true to your values. Their support can be a powerful motivator, helping you to overcome obstacles and keep moving forward on your path to fulfillment.

Ultimately, aligning your actions with your values is about creating a life that resonates with your true self. This alignment not only enhances your sense of purpose but also inspires others around you. As you break free from the mundane and pursue a life of meaning, you become a beacon of motivation for those who seek to ignite their potential. Remember, every small step you take toward alignment is a step toward a more extraordinary life.

Making a Difference in the World

Making a difference in the world begins with recognizing that every small action counts. Many individuals feel overwhelmed by the scale of issues facing society today, but it's essential to understand that change starts with you. By taking even the smallest steps toward positive action, you can contribute to a larger movement that inspires others and creates a ripple effect of goodwill. This realization can ignite a passion within you, pushing you to break free from the monotony of daily life and pursue a more meaningful existence.

Identifying your unique strengths and interests is crucial in this journey. Reflect on what excites you and where your talents lie. Whether it's volunteering, advocating for a cause, or initiating a community project, your skills can be utilized to make a significant impact. Engaging in activities that align with your passions will not only fulfill you but also motivate others to join your mission, fostering a sense of community and shared purpose.

As you embark on this quest to make a difference, surround yourself with like-minded individuals. Building a network of motivated people can enhance your efforts and provide support during challenging times. Share your goals and collaborate on projects that resonate with your mutual interests. This collective energy can amplify your impact, creating a powerful force for change that extends beyond individual efforts.

Embrace the idea that every effort, no matter how small, contributes to the greater good. Celebrate the victories, both big and small, and learn from the setbacks. Each experience will shape your journey and refine your approach, making you more effective in your endeavors. Remember, making a difference is not just about the end result; it's about the growth and transformation you experience along the way.

Finally, remain committed to your purpose and stay open to new opportunities. The world is constantly changing, and as you grow, so too will your ability to impact it positively. Keep seeking ways to inspire others and lead by example. Your dedication to making a difference can motivate those around you to step out of their comfort zones and pursue their own paths of meaningful change. Together, we can create a brighter future for ourselves and for generations to come.

Chapter 11: Reflecting and Reassessing

The Power of Reflection

In the hustle and bustle of our daily lives, we often overlook the immense power of reflection. Taking a moment to pause and evaluate our experiences allows us to gain insights that can lead to significant changes. Reflection is not merely about thinking; it's about understanding our actions, motivations, and the paths we take. By engaging in this practice, we can uncover patterns that may be holding us back from advancing toward our true potential.

One of the greatest benefits of reflection is the clarity it brings. When we step back and analyze our choices, we can identify what truly matters to us. This process helps us distinguish between activities that are merely time-fillers and those that bring genuine fulfillment. By recognizing our core values and passions, we can make more informed decisions that align with our desire for a meaningful life.

Moreover, reflection fosters personal growth by encouraging us to learn from our past experiences. Every success and failure carries lessons that can propel us forward. By reflecting on what we've encountered, we can develop resilience and adaptability. This growth mindset equips us to embrace challenges with confidence, knowing that each experience contributes to our journey of self-improvement.

Another important aspect of reflection is its role in cultivating gratitude. When we take time to contemplate our experiences, we often find moments of joy and learning that we might have missed in the rush of daily life. This gratitude not only enhances our overall well-being but also fuels our motivation to pursue new opportunities. It reminds us that even the mundane can hold meaning if we choose to see it.

Finally, incorporating reflection into our routine can act as a catalyst for change. It empowers us to break free from the ordinary by igniting our passions and ambitions. As we reflect on our desires for a more fulfilling life, we become more attuned to the possibilities around us. By making reflection a regular practice, we can continuously realign ourselves with our goals and aspirations, creating a life that is not just lived but truly experienced.

Adjusting Your Course

Adjusting your course is a vital step in the journey to personal growth and fulfillment. Many individuals find themselves stuck in the monotony of their daily routines, feeling a sense of boredom and dissatisfaction. This often signals a need for change, and recognizing this is the first step toward igniting your potential. Embrace the discomfort that comes with stagnation; it can be a powerful motivator to seek out new paths and experiences.

To effectively adjust your course, it is important to reflect on your current situation and identify what aspects of your life are unfulfilling. Take the time to evaluate your daily activities, relationships, and career choices. Ask yourself what truly brings you joy and meaning. This process of introspection will help you clarify your desires and set the foundation for meaningful change. Remember, the journey toward a more fulfilling life often begins with self-awareness.

Once you have a clearer understanding of what you want, it's time to set actionable goals. These goals should be specific, measurable, and aligned with your newfound insights. Consider breaking them down into smaller, manageable steps to prevent feeling overwhelmed. Creating a roadmap for your journey will not only keep you motivated but also provide a sense of direction as you strive for a life that resonates with your core values.

As you embark on this journey of adjustment, be prepared to face challenges and setbacks. Change can be daunting, but it is also an opportunity for growth. Surround yourself with supportive individuals who encourage your pursuits and share your aspirations. Engaging with a community of like-minded individuals can provide not only motivation but also valuable insights and encouragement as you navigate your new path.

Finally, remember that adjusting your course is not a one-time event but an ongoing process. Life is dynamic, and as you grow, your goals and desires may evolve. Stay flexible and open to new opportunities, and regularly reassess your path. This commitment to continuous growth will not only help you break free from the ordinary but will also lead to a richer, more meaningful life.

Chapter 12: Sustaining Your Momentum

~⁂~

Creating Lasting Habits

Creating lasting habits is essential for anyone looking to break free from the ordinary and ignite their potential. It begins with understanding that change is not a one-time event but a continuous journey. To cultivate meaningful habits, one must first identify the areas of life that feel stagnant or unfulfilling. This self-reflection lays the groundwork for purposeful transformation, allowing individuals to focus on what truly matters to them.

Once you have pinpointed the aspects of your life that require change, the next step is to set clear and achievable goals. These goals act as a roadmap, guiding you through the process of habit formation. It's crucial to start small; rather than trying to overhaul your entire routine at once, focus on integrating one new habit at a time. This incremental approach makes the transition more manageable and increases the likelihood of success.

Accountability plays a vital role in creating lasting habits. Whether it's through a friend, mentor, or a support group, sharing your goals with others can provide the encouragement needed to stay on track. When you know someone is cheering you on, it becomes easier to push through challenges and setbacks. Celebrate your progress, no matter how small, as this reinforces your commitment and fosters a positive mindset.

Incorporating habits into your daily routine requires consistency and patience. Establishing a specific time and place for your new habits can significantly enhance your ability to maintain them. Over time, these repeated actions will become second nature, allowing you to effortlessly integrate them into your life. Remember, perseverance is key; even when motivation wanes, the discipline of sticking to your new habits will keep you moving forward.

Ultimately, creating lasting habits is about aligning your actions with your values and aspirations. As you continuously refine your habits, you will find yourself not only advancing in your personal development journey but also experiencing a profound sense of fulfillment. Embrace the process, remain committed, and watch as your life transforms into something truly meaningful and extraordinary.

Staying Motivated in the Long Run

Staying motivated in the long run can be a challenge, especially for those who feel stuck in their daily routines. The key is to ignite your passion by setting clear and meaningful goals. When you have a vision of what you want to achieve, it becomes easier to push through the obstacles that may arise. A well-defined goal acts as a beacon, guiding you toward the life you desire. Remember, motivation is not just a fleeting feeling; it is a commitment to your growth and development.

To maintain motivation, it is essential to celebrate small victories along the way. Acknowledging these milestones can reinvigorate your spirit and remind you of your progress. Whether it's completing a project, learning a new skill, or simply sticking to your routine, take the time to reflect on your achievements. This practice not only boosts your confidence but also reinforces your dedication to your long-term goals. Celebrate your journey, for every step counts.

Another effective strategy for staying motivated is to surround yourself with positive influences. Engage with individuals who inspire and uplift you. This network of like-minded people can provide encouragement and accountability, making it easier to stay on track. Share your aspirations with them, and they will help you navigate the challenges you may face. Their support can act as an essential catalyst in your pursuit of something more meaningful.

Incorporating variety into your routine can also help sustain your motivation. When monotony sets in, it can be easy to lose sight of your objectives. By introducing new activities, challenges, or learning opportunities, you can keep your mind engaged and excited. Explore different hobbies, take courses, or volunteer in your community. Each new experience enriches your life and reinforces your commitment to personal growth.

Lastly, always remind yourself of the bigger picture. Reflect on why you embarked on this journey in the first place. Your purpose will serve as a powerful motivator during tough times. Write down your reasons, and revisit them when your motivation wanes. Staying connected to your "why" will not only keep you focused but will also empower you to overcome any hurdles in your path. Remember, the journey to a more meaningful life is a marathon, not a sprint, and every effort you invest will bring you closer to your true potential.

Afterword

By the time you reach the last page of a book, you're never the same person who picked it up. I believe the same is true for life. Each chapter, each season, each lesson changes us — sometimes in ways so small we only notice years later, sometimes in ways that knock us flat and force us to rebuild from the ground up.

When I look back, I see a man who made mistakes, who lost his way more times than he cares to admit, but who was blessed with a love that endured and a chance to begin again. I see Molly — steady when I was unsteady, present when I was absent, strong when I was weak. If there's one thread running through all my stories, it is her constancy and the way love has a power greater than my failures.

In *Fake Love*, I tried to show the difference between the fragile and the enduring — the sparks that die out and the flame that keeps burning. In *Love Is What It Is*, I wanted to capture the lessons hiding in plain sight, in the ordinary days that make up most of our lives. And in *Ignite Your Potential*, I shared how those lessons became fuel, turning regret into resilience, giving me a way to live with more purpose and authenticity.

Put together, these three works are not really about me. They are about what connects all of us: our longing to be loved, our struggle to learn, and our hope to live fully. They are reminders that real love doesn't require perfection, only commitment. That wisdom doesn't always arrive with fanfare, but often in quiet, everyday moments. And that potential isn't a gift reserved for a few — it's a spark we all carry, waiting to be lit.

If you take away anything from this bundle, let it be this: you don't have to be flawless to live a meaningful life. You only have to be willing — willing to love honestly, to learn humbly, and to live bravely.

Thank you for walking through these pages with me. My story is only one man's attempt to make sense of his journey, but if it helps you in yours — even in the smallest way — then every word has found its home.

With gratitude and hope,
George Hatcher

About the Author

George Hatcher's life is a testament to resilience, reinvention, and enduring love. With formal schooling that ended in the ninth grade, he built and lost businesses, endured prison sentences, and yet emerged with a new life anchored by his wife of sixty years, Molly.

Drawing from both hardship and redemption, Hatcher writes with unflinching honesty about failure, forgiveness, and the strength of love that lasts. His books combine memoir, reflection, and motivation, offering readers hard-won lessons on resilience, authenticity, and living with purpose.

Now living in Rancho Mirage, California, with Molly, their three cats, and a macaw named Peaches, Hatcher devotes his days to storytelling and reflection. His work continues to prove that beauty isn't found in perfection, but in the courage to repair what is broken and keep moving forward.

Also by George Hatcher

Cool Under Pressure: Warm With Humor

Living Fully While We Wait to Die: Mindfulness Amid Mortality

From Cheers to Tears: The Real Impact of Drinking

Beyond the Scale: Health Benefits of Keto for Wellness

Pages of Passion (Memoir Series, Books 1–4, with more to come)

www.ingramcontent.com/pod-product-compliance
Lightning Source LLC
Chambersburg PA
CBHW071301130626
46556CB00003B/1410